The Art *of* Play

Ignite Your Imagination to
Unlock Insight, Healing and Joy

JOAN STANFORD

SWP

SHE WRITES PRESS

Enjoy! ♡
Joan Stanford

Published 2016
Printed in Canada
ISBN: 978-1-63152-030-3
Library of Congress Control Number: 2016930664

Cover design by Rebecca Lown
Cover image by Catrin Welz-Stein, *Free your Mind*
Interior design by Tabitha Lahr

For information, address:
She Writes Press
1563 Solano Ave #546
Berkeley, CA 94707

She Writes Press is a division of SparkPoint Studio, LLC.

To the child spirit in all of us who is waiting
to be asked to come out and play.

And
To Jeff, Alex and Kate, with love.

Table of Contents: Head Table

Contents

Table of Contents: Head Table

PART 2   Playing With Imagery:
My Life as Raw Material
Poems, Images, Process and Suggestions

Table of Contents: Head Table

There is an old Sanskrit word, *lîla,* which means play. Richer than our word, it means divine play, the play of creation, destruction and re-creation, the folding and unfolding of the cosmos. *Lîla,* free and deep, is both the delight and enjoyment of the moment, and the play of God. It also means love.

Lîla may be the simplest thing there is—spontaneous, childish, disarming. But as we grow and experience the complexities of life, it may also be the most difficult and hard-won achievement imaginable, and its coming to fruition is a kind of homecoming to our true selves.

—Stephen Nachmanovitch

Part 1

Turning Inward: Listening

Every child is an artist. The problem is how to remain an artist when he grows up.

—Pablo Picasso

It took me four years to paint like Raphael but a lifetime to paint like a child.

—Pablo Picasso

Missing Pieces

The Key: Play

This book is about reclaiming what we knew intuitively as children: That life is discovered through the interplay of ourselves and the environment and that the ordinary, everyday world around us is endlessly fascinating. As children we see, hear, smell and touch making "sense" of our experiences. Anyone who has been around a baby witnesses their hands and feet constantly wriggling then finding their way to the mouth. Soon grabbing at anything and everything within reach happens, and what is grabbed also travels quickly to the mouth. We are eager to ingest the world as new arrivals. As toddlers we pay attention: fascinated by the journey of an ant along a leaf, a ladybug on a petal. We are open, alive, sensate. We giggle; we are joyful. Each day is an adventure as we learn through exploring and experimenting. Each day we learn through play. Play is our very nature.

We play with whatever is at hand. A stick becomes a sword, a spoon a musical instrument. Our imaginations create realities that we inhabit. And when offered crayons or paints, we choose a color that excites us and use it over and over. There is joy in the process, less concern with product.

What happens to this joy? Where does our delight in play go? I believe it is slowly forced underground as our education becomes head-centered and less experiential. We learn from others and begin to place our trust "out there" instead of "in here." We disconnect from our innate creativity. What also happens is a silencing of our inner knowing. Yet that voice lives inside us waiting for us to listen.

Listening

CHAPTER 1

Listening

I began to listen to what Carl Jung called that "still, small voice within" entering mid-life. I even became an art therapist to encourage others to find ways to connect to that voice and allow it expression. That voice is a whisper; that voice is shy. But not always: Sometimes that voice is so hungry for expression that it explodes on the page or paper in dramatic fashion. More often, though, it needs tender coaxing to emerge from hiding. For after many years of being ignored, criticized, even ridiculed, the voice retreats to safety. I believe this voice holds insights that we need to hear and, most importantly, honor and share. I believe this voice speaks from our essence, our core self, our soul. This voice connects us to the Great Mystery, to a wisdom inside each of us, to life unfolding. And I believe creative play is the key to unlock that treasure.

> *"When the soul wants something to be known, she throws out an image in front of her and steps into it."*
> —Meister Eckhart

This book fulfills a promise I made to myself, with some prompting from others, to honor my poems and images, **the expressions of my explorations through creative play.** As much as I preached, I failed to practice. Scribbled on scraps, many poems were shoved into journals or drawers. While the voice was heard it was not honored. Similarly, collages were rarely framed or hung but stacked and hidden in piles. When an image impresses someone with its honesty I tell them to put it up, view it daily. This allows the message to deepen and enter consciousness more fully.

As I selected the poems and images for this book I realized that the book also needed to honor the transformational journey that created them. How did I move from a stance of claiming, "But I am not creative" and "But I have no time" to a place of willingness to explore, to play? What encouraged me to listen, to attend to these fragmented whispers within? Discovering my voice was a huge opening for me and quite literally saved my life. I hope to inspire you as others have inspired me with their heartfelt words and images, to turn your ear inward and to play. My message is: If I can do this, anyone can. I have absolute faith that you, too, can experience your life expanded and enriched through this process.

We do not have to retreat to a mountaintop. We do not have to take art classes. We do not have to change our priorities and our schedules. We only have to pay attention to the moments and tasks of our everyday life through creative reflection, to connect to our inner self and to receive these whispers that are so meaningful. To not demand that they show up whole, with a label and a readily apparent message. **To play with imagery; to listen to what wants to be heard. This inner voice** is a powerful ally on our journey through life.

CHAPTER 2

But I Am Not Creative

If you have already felt a slight trepidation at being asked to creatively reflect, let me reassure you that this is exactly where I started. My approach to creativity now is: We are all inherently creative; creative expression, in whatever way, is enlivening and healing. **Play opens the door.** Throughout history, cross-culturally, societies have integrated art making into rituals to bridge the spiritual and material realms, the personal and the universal. Today, in our culture, the marketplace has largely hijacked art, and most of us feel disconnected from our birthright of creativity.

Images are powerful: just think of advertising. We each have a personal storehouse of imagery that, when tapped into, informs and offers insights not otherwise available. This is not about becoming a famous artist or a published writer (although that may indeed happen). This is not about impressing others but expressing yourself to yourself. It is about listening **and playful exploration**.

I invite the child in you to come out and play, as children, quite naturally, have active imaginations and delight in creating. Play is such an essential part of creativity. When we play we let go of many rules, many "shoulds." Anything goes. We horse around. We become horses . . . and tigers, superheroes, villains, princesses, doctors. We try on roles. We pretend. The Latin root of pretend is *tendere*, which means to stretch, to extend, to proceed.

Adults experience play more as work. Playing a sport is different than free play. Some companies now recognize the value of freeing up creativity and use brainstorming to help people think outside the box. Free association asks the censor to step aside. Participants are encouraged to blurt things out, to be spontaneous, silly even. Childish. The key is withholding judgment.

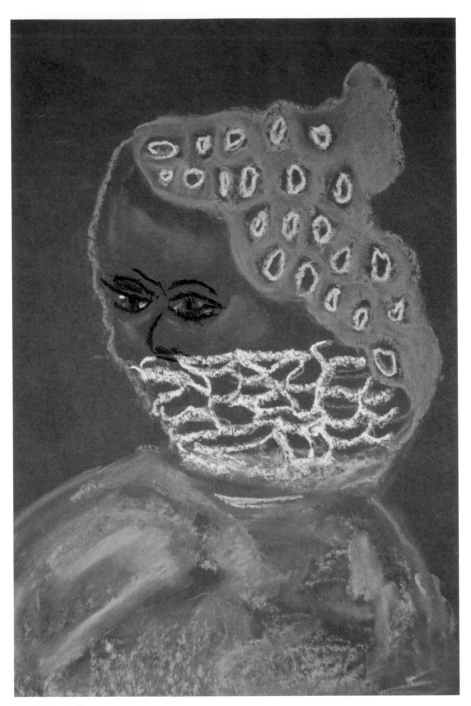

Silenced

Unfortunately, even children learn all too soon to compare. "I am not creative" implies compared to a "real" artist. Our self-critical voice dampens our impulse to create and makes it no longer fun. The delight we had in the ***process*** of experimenting with materials, in the ***process*** of discovering something new is replaced by an emphasis on the end product. To reenter this vast world within you, trusting the importance of process is a dramatic shift. I encourage you to override the inhibitions drummed into you and allow yourself this gift of expression. **Allow yourself to reclaim that lost delight.** Remember this is just for you. There is no right or wrong way to do it. Release your expectations of realism, rationality or neatness. Invite your child self to come out and play.

Coming apart at my "seems"

CHAPTER 3

My Beginnings

How did I begin my journey? At midlife, in the midst of a full and busy life, I felt a sense of self-alienation. I had an eerie sense of going through the motions but felt slightly removed as though I had lost something important. The life I had crafted with its roles of wife, mother, businesswoman and community member began to disintegrate. After suffering a personal loss, I felt disconnected and fragmented. From the outside my life appeared fine, perfect even: I was innkeeping with my husband in a beautiful place; I had two wonderful young children; I was actively involved in my work and my community. Yet on the inside I felt I was coming apart at the seams. "Seams" is the perfect word for what "seems" to be the case is not always what is: My "seems" were coming apart.

In this state I experienced true separateness. I felt ashamed of my feelings. How self-indulgent, I thought. "Get over it," I scolded myself. In fact, I was pushing the pause button.

Any number of events can cause this pause: a health crisis, a move, a family problem, a love affair, or a death. Whatever it is that occasions our stepping back or stepping out of the daily momentum of our lives also offers an opportunity to reflect, to look deeply inside ourselves. If taken, this opportunity, although created by a deep disconnect, can lead to a deeper connection to self and our way forward.

At this critical time my children were taking piano lessons from a woman who was an expressive arts therapist. They drew and painted as well as learned piano pieces. Something intrigued me about their time with her. Instead of dropping them off, rushing to run errands and returning to pick them up, I began to wait in her forest sanctuary. A few lines from a poem I later wrote speaks of this unwinding, the sense of shifting gears that is so necessary for mindful reflection:

Leaving the main road,
Entering the twisted path,
Slowing down,
Slowing way down,
I park,
Move into the dark
Small among towering trees. (from "Return")

This stopping of my normal flow was the first step. The second was actually telling this therapist that I envied my kids this time with her. She told me she had adult beginners and I signed on to learn piano, something I had never done in my life. Little did I know I was beginning a journey that continues today. I began to listen, amid the busy buzz of my ongoing life, to myself. **I began to return**.

CHAPTER 4

Reclaiming the Child

Early on in working with her (we often began at an art table with some conversation) she asked me, "What is your greatest fear?" I said to have a child go missing. She suggested creating a poster like the ones in the post office for the missing child part of me. So being a good student I went home and on a piece of newsprint, using a child's watercolors set, I painted *Missing*, positioning the watery letters at the top. Then the face of a young girl emerged. After sitting and taking in this image, I wrote a poem.

MISSING

Where is the child
With wide rainbow eyes,
Apple cheeks,
Crescent moon barrettes,
In sunshine hair?

Where is the child
Afloat in the world,
A bubble bouncing,
A star beam glowing,
A dandelion dancer
With fluff-puff shoes?

Where is the child
Of wishes and wonder,
Of longing and looking,
Running and skipping,
Singing and swinging,
And playing with days?

Where is the child
Of purple and red?
Asleep? Or dead?
An adult instead?

What I was missing as an adult was the lightness and delightedness with which I greeted each day as a child. **I was no longer "playing with days" but hurrying through to-do lists.** I don't mean to over-romanticize childhood, but I needed to recognize the weight my responsibilities had added and how my attitude had shifted to one of resistance and resentment. I address this further in Part 2.

CHAPTER 5

Materials Don't Matter

I learned materials didn't matter. Taking the time to sit quietly and attend to my own impulses was all I needed. I remember scribbling during a power outage:

THOUGHTS BY THE LIGHT OF AN OIL LAMP

It's not the pen.
    Still . . .
What words I could write
               if I had a quill.
It's not the light.
    Though . . .
Predawn, with moon and stars
Seems most right.
It's not the room.
    But…
A book-lined den
With fireplace
Would surely inspire
My dried-up pen.
When you get right down to it
It's none of these.

It's getting right down to it
Writing it down.
In the end
It's just beginning.

Not having specific materials need not be an obstacle. Abandon this excuse. Play with what is at hand: markers, crayons, even pencils. Later you may want more variety. I recommend having a box of oil pastels, a box of chalk pastels, a set of watercolors and different types of papers. I had a large-size pad of newsprint to encourage free play as well as a pad of paper from an art store. For collaging anything can be used: magazine images, photographs, newspapers, tissue paper, wrapping paper, ribbons, fabric, different textures and objects. Your imagination will lead you. A simple notebook will do for writing.

CHAPTER 6

But I Have No Time: Meeting Our Resistance

The number-one excuse for so many things: I have no time. But be honest, if you want something, you find the time. I remember hearing a joke that if you ever wanted to attack cleaning a closet or any procrastinated project, simply say that you are going to sit down and write. The cleanest house is often that of a writer on deadline. We find many ways to avoid spending time with ourselves and making something **even** when we know the value of it and tell ourselves that this making is what we want to do. This resistance is an interesting place to begin. You might try drawing that part of you that denies, impedes, blocks your own creativity. What words are being thrown at you? Does the voice remind you of anyone?

I feel we have both an inner cheerleader and an inner naysayer or saboteur. I find it helpful to have a conversation with these parts, especially our naysayer. I often learn something about my own reluctance that allows me to move through a block.

An example:
Welcome Naysayer. Haven't seen you for a while.
Naysayer (N): I am always here.
Joan (J): You seem to make your presence known when I am trying to accomplish something.
N: I remind you of your past failures.
J: You make me feel bad. You tell me I'll never finish, that I start but don't follow through. Why must you undermine me?

N: I am here to protect you.

J: From what?

N: From humiliating yourself, by failing.

J: But you stop me from succeeding by not helping me try. You dismantle my commitment.

N: You are taking a risk showing yourself this way. I don't want you to feel how inadequate you are or to feel rejected.

J: But you make me feel inadequate.

N: Yes, but it is different when others judge you.

J: But I really want to do this and you're making it so hard. I want to try. I believe this is important.

N: You have to believe harder. Maybe you need to tell me I can trust you with this.

J: You can trust me with this. I can handle it. I will be OK.

N: We'll see.

J: Thank you for caring and protecting me but really, I'm good. Can you please be silent or help me?

N: I am helping. You are becoming more committed each day.

J: But I don't enjoy this struggle. Perhaps you can help me later but for now, can you wait outside?

I check in with this part often and if I'm feeling strong, I'll let him know. Notice how this is a "he." Once, in a drawing, I depicted this part of me as a wigged and robed judge sitting on high, perhaps an early internalized vision of a harsh God.

In beginning this book, I did a drawing.

Container for My Words

I wanted to create a container for my words so I drew a vessel. This odd entity arose to the left and I immediately recognized my shadow, my saboteur. I countered with a scribble and saw a seated woman holding her heart, protecting my offering. I then added the golden balloon and saw this as releasing my book to the world.

Holding and Releasing

When I am stuck in writing, I bring out these images to remind me of process; **to remind me to play, to be loose, less judgmental, more trusting.** The dialogue is on-going between these two aspects: the desire to express and share vs. my own resistance, the fear of being seen, hurt.

But back to the question of making the time once we have confronted our own internal resistance.

I remember reading on a card "Time is all we have." This statement caused me to stop telling myself that I had no time. I realized what I really meant by saying that was specific to doing something, e.g., "I have no time to go for a walk." The focus shifts to intention: What do I intend to use my time for? In my busy life, this "no time" complaint was huge.

My point is that often the "no time" excuse is really suspect. So back to "just begin" . . . believe something will happen. Yes, but for a busy person how to just begin?

This collage depicts a woman racing against time. I really felt like this rat, as if my life was a race. I never had enough time. I always had a sense of rushing.

Rat Race

This collage shows the opposite, the idealized centered, balanced, unencumbered person, mindfully walking her path.

Idealized Centered Self

This third collage represents the challenge, the struggle to find balance.

Balancing Time

I do have to accept the confines that time imposes, but I hold in my hands the scales. I actually created a collage journal on the theme of time and received many insights about time. The most important being "It is about time to . . ." The phrase "Make the most of time" became an imperative to make time, so with snippets of minutes here and there I "made" time.

Time Journal, cover

Time Journal, inside front cover: Hands of Time

Time Journal, side view

Time Journal, inside back cover: Time Is in My Hands

I am encouraging you to understand that setting aside even a few minutes is a valid beginning. Just a few minutes, just a line or two will start the change. Just stating the desire is forming an intention. Again the root is *tendere*; here it is, a stretching toward, taking aim. In fairy-tales, someone is often offered three wishes. These must be summoned from within. The power is in the naming of the wish, in formulating what is truly, deeply wanted: creating the intention.

In *Art Is A Way of Knowing*, Pat Allen writes about intention as a way of invoking the creative force or spirit to assist in our explorations. True commitment garners unseen help. Then the will follows and manifests the wish or intent through action. Once I could admit to myself that I needed and wanted some quiet time and space, I began seizing minutes. Like a thirsty person being offered water, these sips became gulps.

And I was a busy woman. As an innkeeper, there is no nine-to-five schedule, or evenings, weekends, or holidays off. We lived in our business and our business lived in us. As mentioned, I had two young children, pets, staff, a husband and community interests. At some point I recognized that just as on an airplane when we are instructed to place the oxygen mask on our face before helping our children, I needed to feed my inner self to be of service to others.

CHAPTER 7

How to Begin: Stop, Look and Listen

If my story of a fast-paced life resonates, I would suggest the best way for you to begin is to stop, look and listen. Find a way to step back. If you can find an expressive arts therapist all the better, but taking time out of your busy schedule to simply be with your own thoughts and feelings is a start. Make the time to listen to yourself, to play. Put hand to paper with writing or art making to allow expression of these thoughts and feelings. Open the door. Try not to set up unrealistic goals, which if not met will sabotage you with a sense of failure. It is helpful to commit to some small doable thing, perhaps a line a day or a doodle. Or scan a magazine for an image that jumps out for you. Create an idea box. But the main thing is to begin and continue.

Start noticing what impresses you as you move through your day. If you notice an elderly, stooped couple holding hands and this catches your attention, jot it down or do a drawing. It doesn't have to be a realistic sketch, just some expression to capture what you felt or what image was evoked. Or you might have an angry response to something. Represent that energy or explore the trigger and the arc of emotional buildup and release with color, shape or a line. Maybe you see sunlight on a cobweb or hear birdsong or smell jasmine. Start noticing and noting. The magnet I spotted on a friend's refrigerator provided an excellent frame for reflection. It read: "What surprised me today? What inspired me today? What moved me today?" Be more receptive to objects around you, perhaps sensing metaphoric connections to items that attract you. For me, I began collecting feathers.

Make your practice realistic. Find what works best with your life. Allow yourself some flexibility—enough to forgive lapses, but not too much—or you will break the connection and weaken your commitment.

We find so many ways to avoid time for personal reflection, or what I like to call self check-ins. Some of us are never disconnected from our devices and Sunday is no longer a separate, peaceful retreat day. If they are not there already, we can create external distractions. And as discussed, our internal chatter is a constant challenge. Yet the benefits are worth the effort. I want to stress that even if you feel you have no time and no artistic ability, this process of taking a few moments out of your day to reflect with writing and art making helps you connect to your own life and to life as a whole with new insights. Your inner wisdom will whisper to you.

CHAPTER 8

How My Life Changed

"Our own life is the instrument with which we experiment with truth."

—Thich Nhat Hanh,

My crisis was essentially a crisis of meaning. As my assumptions about many things fell into a tailspin, I searched for answers to existential questions. How do I learn to love this life I am given? How can I make peace with internal conflicts, with my own vulnerability and the mystery of life itself with loss and change as givens? A friend once related a Sufi story of someone encountering a crippled man. The cripple had no legs and was scooting along the ground, ragged and dirty but with a wonderful, huge smile on his face. The other person questioned, "Why are you smiling?" The cripple replied, "What's my choice?" Of course, there is choice, but I wanted to find my capacity to smile. I wanted to savor the moments of life, to say, "yes" to what the moments of my life present. I have always loved Mary Oliver's poem "When Death Comes" which concludes by her wanting to have lived her life as "a bride married to amazement"-an image of open-hearted receptivity and as a bridegroom embracing the world-an image of active engagement.

These words suggest that the child wonder we began our life journey with can be a chosen attitude. In fact, this wonder is an essential antidote to the cynicism that experience of the world can breed. The armor we installed as disappointments and disillusionments battered our young imagining selves also deadens. We can sleepwalk through our days, anesthetized by routines, unconscious of anything amazing. Yet *being* itself becomes more amazing as we mature, as we deepen and ripen our souls through broadened awareness of all we don't know. We can embody the curiosity of a child in exploring our own unconscious and the mystery of life itself.

Stephen Nachmanovitch, in *Free Play*, writes:

> *In dealing with unconscious mind, we're dealing with an ocean full of rich, invisible life forms swimming underneath the surface. In creative work we're trying to catch one of these fish; but we can't kill the fish, we have to catch it in a way that brings it to life. In a sense we bring it amphibiously to the surface so it can walk around visibly; and people will recognize something familiar because they've got their own fish who are cousins to your fish.*

To be this open-armed bride with openhearted acceptance requires my recognizing my place in some larger story. If I am to be fully present in life with all its changes and shifts, I must realize that I see only part of the picture at any one time. I need to be conscious of what is invisible. When I am able to see each piece of my life as connected, to see an ending as also a beginning, my stance to change changes. While I am powerless to stop time and events that occur, I do have choices and those choices create how I live my life. I can chose to be amazed or dismayed or both; I can bury or express my feelings; I can be open or closed. These choices require an awareness that is enhanced by exploring the rich, invisible world within.

As I pay more attention to the moments, interactions and impressions of my daily life, exploring them through creative process, I experience a fundamental shift. I relate differently to my husband, my children, my coworkers, my friends and myself. I can be more present to what is truly happening by being more aware of my internal messages. Within, my judgments, projections and ideas about how I should respond create static interference that, once I am aware of, can be tuned out or dialed down. Since I partially create the reality I exist within through my own projections, assumptions and responses, using my creativity to reshape and explore these aspects is powerful. I am reminded again of fairy-tales. Often the child is offered a magic wand with special abilities. In art making, the magic wand is the imagination. Just as a magic wand can make things appear or disappear, my thoughts and beliefs have the power to create or transform outer aspects of my life.

Awareness allows a space to open up to receive more fully the moments of my life. I see with new eyes through the re-visioning I do through creative process. This in turn allows a shift from resistance and resentment of aspects of my life to an attitude of gratitude.

Fr. William Rewak, author of *The Right Taxi*, in an interview in *Santa Clara magazine* writes:

> *"The things we touch and see and hear are signs of a deeper reality. And not only signs, they carry with them the spark of creation and grace that fires everything. We need not look to sunsets, or the morning whistling of the wind, to find poetry; it's also in the pens and pencils on my desk, the pictures on my wall, the needles I use to sew buttons on my old sweater."*

Essentially, relating to the everyday, to the ordinary moments of our lives with a sense of wonder opens our eyes to the extraordinariness of existence.

Again, Fr. Rewak:

> *". . . it's the very nature of a poem (and I would add, image) to be a sign, to lead us to further meaning, to see what we have not seen before, to note that* **the dust of reality has flecks of gold in it**. *So that the creation of a poem is itself a prayer, an acknowledgement and praise of something or someone, lying at the heart of our experience."*
> *(emphasis author's)*

I came to see those "flecks of gold" as playful art making opened my eyes.

CHAPTER 9

Expressive Arts Process: Imaginative Play

While I had journaled off and on since high school, the idea of expressing myself with art was totally foreign and intimidating. Like those gallery rooms in museums not open to the general public, with a velvet cord stretching across the entry, I felt I had to keep out. This world was reserved for those with talent and training, a members-only club from which I was excluded.

What I learned was that expressive arts therapy is a dynamic, non-verbal approach to self-discovery that anyone can use. A novice may actually have an advantage in not having any preconceived ideas or expectations. Using different modalities, through writing, art making, movement, dance and music, we are invited to explore beneath our social selves to discover inner truths.

Facing the blank paper we are asked to make a mark, a mark of any kind as long as it is our own. Another follows. Images, lying dormant in our hearts and heads, appear before us. We may shade, highlight, distort or blur. We may add perspective. Through the doing we experience the very nature of our larger walking life: first this, then that. Just begin, often with no idea of how or where, but just place that mark on the blank page; take that first step. Add, subtract, wash over, reject, love, balance, crowd, flip-flop. As we free energy that has become trapped, stuck, we move toward expressing and seeing our truth. We open spaces. And we give form, which, in turn, informs. We invite relationship; we receive information. We may be totally surprised by what appears, feeling as though some entity other than ourselves created it. Our curiosity is aroused.

The process is empowering because we are actively engaged; we are the agents of change. In manipulating colors, shapes and designs we are exercising decision-making. We are making choices from a world of possibilities. If we allow ourselves, we are experiencing the pleasure of playing with materials. Nothing is fixed or finished until we decide to stop. We are the rule makers and the rule breakers. How liberating!

There is also the power of seeing something we have only felt or imagined immediately reflected back to us. Once a participant in a support group for cancer caregivers that I was co-leading refused to draw how she was feeling. She was totally resistant to the idea but finally acquiesced and chose a large sheet of black paper. She took a marker and placed, rather forcefully, a dot in the corner. The rest of the group responded by admitting they felt exactly like her "picture." She had captured how alone, tiny and overwhelmed many felt as they cared for a loved one with cancer. As they dealt with medical issues, bureaucracies and emotions, both theirs and those of their loved one, they felt lost in a black uncertainty. They struggled to be that light in the darkness.

I understand this resistance. At first, I didn't even trust that I had any "inner" voice that wanted to be heard. But knowing my outside remained the same while on the inside I was in turmoil suggested otherwise. As I played with art making, my images continually surprised, amazed, delighted and frightened me. I became more conscious.

Becoming conscious is about rediscovering, uncovering and re-owning associations and personal meanings.

Some techniques that aid in this are dialoging with images. Asking two colors or two parts of a drawing to speak to one another can be instructive. This can be playful, for example, "Let's just see if old Mr. Bump on a Log has something to say about Free as a Bird Balloon Face." When a being or symbol appears, we can also engage in conversation. Sometimes writing with the nondominant hand for the voice of the image is enlightening.

Here is an example of the power of this process from three simple drawings I did and wrote about while completing my master's degree (which is in psychology, with an art therapy emphasis).

I faced the blank page and felt as empty as that space before me. I picked up a blue oil pastel marker and drew a shape that became a teardrop. I thought: I want to go inside the tear. As I said this to myself, tears came and I recognized this as an old wound that has left empty spaces in my heart. I saw a tiny, black, mask-shaped button a fellow student had given me on the table and placed it on another sheet of paper and drew it. There was no black marker in my box so I used blue again, then opened another box to add black. Black and blue. I hurt. The mask hurts. I spoke again: I want to pierce the mask.

I started another page with the idea of a garden. I was still holding the blue marker so I drew a blue line and blue seeds. I heard, "plant blue seeds" and felt this meant transforming my sadness, my blueness, my tears. The images led me through this process. I decided to dialogue.

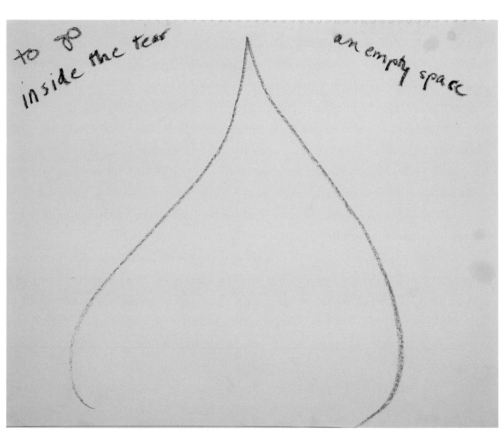

Blue Flame (first image)

Joan (J): Welcome image. Do you have a name?

Image (I): Blue Flame. You drew me as a teardrop but I am a flame. Remember the fire in the water.

J: You mean energy in my sadness?

I: Yes. I mean purification by feeling, distillation through heat to essence as in spirit, pure being.

J: In looking at you, I see empty space as fullness.

I: You know this, Joan. You know fullness; you are discovering the fullness of empty.

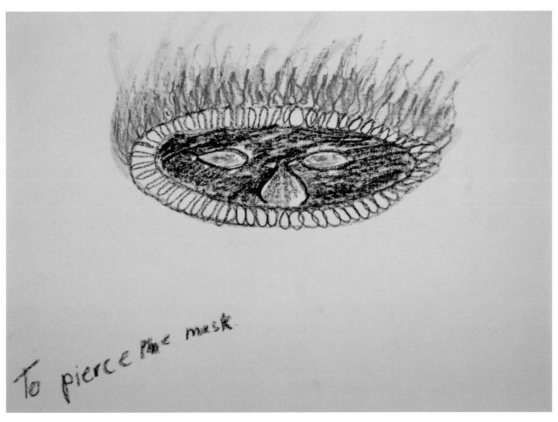

Mask-Shaped Button (second image)

Then I speak to the second image.

J: Welcome image. You remind me of Inuit art.

I: I bring the knowing of cold, frigid places where the heart hides.

J: Are you related to Blue Flame?

I: Yes, I want you to add blue flames to my edges.

J: OK. This is empowering to do. I feel your eyeholes; I sense cool fire burning behind the mask.

(I breathe. I rub the colors together, and the little mask, the model, which is on the paper above my drawing, flips over.)

I: You are willing to pierce the mask. Remember I am a half mask. Your face is always present, too.

J: My mouth is exposed. I can speak. My heart-speak. My truth.

I: You need to know this.

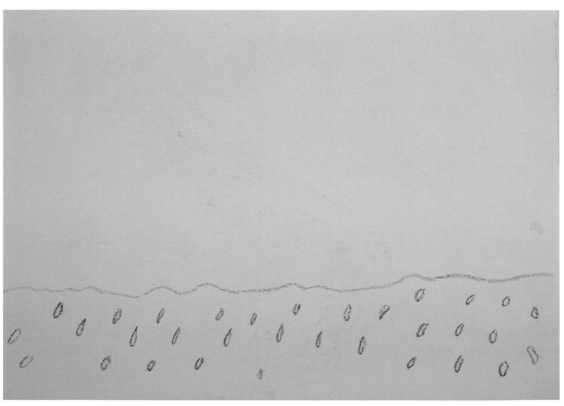

Blue Seeds (third image)

I dialogue with the third image.

J: Welcome image. I feel you as barren.

I: I am not barren. I am fertile ground. I am the ground of becoming. The blue garden you will grow. I am the ocean, your feeling, unconscious world. I am vast, unlimited. You are ready to explore the fertility of this place. No, I am not barren.

J: I feel the frigid northland. If I tip you upside down I see snow falling. I sense the silence, the stillness. I feel the crisp, fresh, pure crystals. I remember each snowflake is unique.

I: You have fear of melting to feeling. Do not cut yourself off from your fire. Your flame is blue, pure.

J: I need to allow my feelings.

I: Trust yourself. You know what to do.

Another example of the healing of splits also involved this process of staying with the image. I made a chalk pastel in response to a Halloween theme, "What would I want to be?" I began drawing black zigzag lines to create a two-sided clown image: one black, one white. The drawing evolved into a being with creature feet and creature hands; the white side feels reptilian, frog-like. When I rotated the image I saw an animal running. This seems to suggest transformation, so I wanted to learn more.

J: Welcome image. You are a surprise.

I: I am a shape-shifter. I am not a mask or a costume. I am about being real.

J: You are black and white. You seem open, not solid.

I: My black side has spaces, too, white spaces, just as my white side has dark holes. What you call open on one side is the color of dense on the other.

J: I feel this is cerebral and missing the point.

I: You think and feel. Your thinking is felt; your feeling is thoughtful. You are waging a war, heart vs. head, which you have already won.

J: I need to feel this.

I: You need to trust. Look in my eyes. Burning coals, clear seeing. My face is bird-like. I am amphibian: of the land, of the water, of the air. You are body, feeling and spirit. You will know this more and more. You are many parts. You are real.

J: Thank you.

Shape-Shifter

I learned to use metaphors that I spoke aloud as starting points; for example, "I'm in a rut." As I drew, I could determine how deep it was, how wide and what was around. How might I escape?

I found it so wonderful to be asking, "What if . . ." and letting myself explore rather than bemoaning, "Why?" **Questions invited explorations, expansions widening my lens of perception. I could live with unanswerable questions, the mystery of not knowing.**

Mark Nepo, in *Seven Thousand Ways to Listen*, writes:

> *"How do we listen and stay in conversation with all that is beyond our awareness? Many aspects of living continually bring us into this conversation: curiosity, pain, wonder, loss, beauty, truth, confusion, and fresh experience"* . . . and *" to limit existence to only what we know blinds us to the mystery of how we are all connected."*

Paul Klee said, "Art is making the strange familiar and the familiar strange."

I often see the expressive arts as a tree with deep roots and branches extended wide. The process is grounded as we use our bodies and concrete materials, yet we are accessing the unconscious realm below the surface. The trunk grows thick as we release energy. We reconnect to the flowing nature of all life, the sap. The branches allow connection and communication with self and other, allowing compassion to spread. Feelings are made visible. The individual can connect to the transpersonal spiritual realm and rediscover a sense of true belonging in mystery.

CHAPTER 10

My Process: Play

My process became writing and art making, usually the two together, supporting and expanding one another. Sometimes the drawing evoked the writing, as in "Missing." Sometimes the writing became the voice of the collage as in "Meeting the Crone." I often invited the images to speak as discussed above.

Collage, an art form that combines existing images, fragments, shapes, textures and objects into a new presentation, became my preferred activity. I love the process of collage and the freedom it offers me, an untrained artist, to create with images. Scanning what is at hand, I notice what stimulates, pleases, intrigues, attracts, repels or, perhaps, scares. This is intuitive stimulus response; I try to remain as open as possible and do not look for specific images but rather allow the images to find me. I suspend judgment as much as possible also, so that my logical discriminating mind does not dismiss a rusted piece of metal as junk, thus inhibiting my poetic impulse from re-viewing it as a heart shape with a corroded hole. The process is playful and invites the child self to step in, as the controlling, rational adult self steps aside. Because such materials are readily available and plentiful, trial and error is encouraged. There is none of the pressure to be careful that is imposed by other more costly and precious media. As I experiment spontaneity enters, loosening me up.

Collage replicates dreaming as non-linear and illogical combinations are made. I can place the starry night sky inside a wide, open mouth. I can place my body inside a whale or become the whale by putting my face on its body. As in dreams, I can fly, animals can talk and no rules apply. I allow myself to be taken over by the materials, to change directions, and this is enlivening, exciting. I cut out, move things around on the page many times, creating and adjusting relationships between shapes, colors, etc.

What image wants to be center stage? What image do I always find in my hand, unable to fit in? Sometimes as I turn over a piece to glue, I decide to use the reverse side instead. Process leads and shifts occur. I paste when I feel satisfied. As images are evocative, I discover new connections.

When I collage, I journey. I never know the destination when I start out. Seemingly random assortments constellate into a finished piece. Each is a little mystery open to multiple interpretations. They suggest but do not completely tell a story, to which the viewer is invited to add his or her own experience. Each story is complete and yet only a part of a much larger story.

Collage is also the perfect metaphor for life, mirroring how we create our lives. We take fragments and piece something together. We cut out; we fill in. In integrating a variety of pieces, many totally mismatched, we fashion a hybrid. Each day brings more material to be integrated and we are never done with the past. Collage contains both; the used and the new. We move beyond simplistic notions of one thing excluding another. Multilayered, collage serves as a container for a myriad of impressions.

My life as an innkeeper at the time I began my journey was enmeshed, with no clear boundaries between work and home or my roles of wife and business partner. Life felt chaotic with many demands vying for my attention. Collage, the process of disassembling and then reassembling, was the perfect medium for me during disintegration, exploration and re-integration. Like the inn, within my life were many doors, each one a world within a whole. I realized that I needed to separate them. Just as in collaging I can isolate one aspect of something—an eye out of a face, a sentence out of a paragraph, a phrase out of a sentence, or a letter out of a word—I needed to focus my attention by isolating aspects of my life. This allowed me to honor each piece. As in meditation, there is a quieting of the mind from busy background to essence. As I attend to the present moment before me I am better able to act with intention and clarity.

This process also made apparent how each piece contributed to the whole, the connections between the pieces and the relative importance of each. This was healing for me, as I needed to step out, to see how better to fit in. The many pieces off my life could be overwhelming. Collaging created peace.

In collage, as in life, I struggle and I stop. I stumble, quit, change directions. I step back. Something happens: a surprise, an accident, nothing at all, blankness. I become curious, engaged again or I sit apart feeling my separation. Things that unfold reveal what I would rather deny and avoid. Playful art making takes me again and again to the edge of beginning, to the place of choice. I discover that magic is not something extraordinary but the seeing of the extraordinary in the ordinary. It is not to make art but to see the art in all things and to know we are each a part of that art: the art of nature and the Great Mystery.

Being present to the changing and rearranging collage that is life, to the ebb and flow of being, is the gift I receive from this practice. My highs and lows are connected as two points on the same wave. Asking questions and giving thanks for my place in the mystery matters more than receiving answers. In fact, I become wary of answers. Instead I learn to trust myself, the flow and the bigger picture. What a relief to set down the burden of "getting it right!" I don't have to do this all alone; there *is* community. I *can* ask for help. I can abandon some unspoken hope that if I do it right or best, I will receive some reward, or at least avoid some harsh punishment.

These insights occurred through my personal explorations and within the context of classes and peer groups. At this time I also was part of a woman's group in my community that met twice monthly to share our creative selves. Since making art is a solo activity, it is wonderful to be able to interact with other like-minded people. The support, encouragement and cross-fertilization are invaluable.

Erik Erikson writes that the last task in life is achieving integrity: "This consists in bringing together in a meaningful story our past and present and in reconciling ourselves with the approaching end of life." The elder person must also arrive at an understanding of his/her integration into a larger story, a continuing story. This allows connection instead of despair. Collage also makes me aware of interrelationships beyond this space and time. The collage process honors the transitory by employing objects or images from the past. The collage created serves as witness, enshrining experience.

Through the **process** of collage making, in playing with the papers, letting images speak to me, I began some interesting conversations.

I encourage you to experiment with different ways of creating this conversation. Through writing and art making, I began a journey that is ongoing.

| CHAPTER 11 |

Life as Art/Life as Play

"All the arts we practice are apprenticeship. The big art is our life."
—M.C. Richards

"The object of art is to give life shape."
—Jean Anouilh

While this journey was/is playful, it is also intensely serious. Creative expression impacts the way I live my life in significant ways. I created the following chart to demonstrate my before and after tendencies.

BEFORE	AFTER
wishing	willing
waiting	beginning
passive	active
goal-oriented	process-oriented
judging	accepting
why?	why not and what and how?

(continued on next page)

BEFORE	AFTER
what do they want/need?	what do I want/need?
doing it right	exploring/experimenting/no right/wrong
either/or thinking	both/and coexist
sorrow as negative/punitive	sorrow as connecting/opening
closeted, hiding, withholding	out in the open, being seen
fear of failure	delight in trying
shame	aliveness
guilt	gratitude
silence/frozen	voice/flowing
seeking approval	letting go/trusting
victim	participant

What I experience now is that these tendencies themselves are coexisting. What is critical is my awareness of the continuum, of where I am on it and the choices I can make because of this awareness. Now that I allow that process, i.e., movement back and forth, I experience freedom. I see how allowing myself and others this freedom is a choice. In playful art making, I practiced this freedom as I allowed myself choices: I added this, not that; I felt intense so used intense colors; I used water or ignored the water; I stayed inside the lines or boundary of the page or I went off the edges; I cut up and tore. I became my own censor and sensor.

Just as in art making, I am now creating my life moment by moment. I can accept or resist, compare or dare, borrow and copy. I pay attention to my perceptions, sift and sort, follow what pulls at something inside me. Today may be very different from yesterday and tomorrow. I allow this, too. I am drawing the circle larger and larger to include more: both the desired and the not desired, to join rather than disown, to discover the ability to love what is.

So many of us seek enlightenment and the true meaning of life with a new urgency as we age, as assumed roles fall away, and we glimpse death ahead. We may be conditioned to look elsewhere, to others for answers. Yet teachers and philosophers from Socrates to Jesus have advised, know thyself, look within. Creative process invites the "within" to have a voice and a face—one that is now heard and seen on the page. While I am an innkeeper, I am no longer an "in"-keeper and appreciate how critical it is to discover and express our own truths.

Turning our ear inward to listen to our soul's voice and then representing that conversation offers a mirror from which we can all benefit. This book represents my explorations through that process and offers one mirror. The poems and images speak to different parts of my journey: disintegration, searching, paying attention, seeing differently, responding, connecting, letting go, accepting death, gratitude, belonging. Since I have been emphasizing the importance of process over product, I also include notes on my process in creating the pieces. A conversation, a quote, an incident, a question, a feeling—anything might prompt my playing with art supplies and/or words. I also offer suggestions for you to explore.

You can picture me writing at a messy table, often with a candle. I learned to trust that if I sat still and listened, the whispers would come. In the beginning, I wrote in the car, waiting to pick up my kids, because at that point I didn't have a practice or a studio but would write when I had a solitary moment or an urge to understand something. The more I did, the more I valued the process. Now I create image journals in small, 6-inch-by-6-inch spiral-bound books with the image on the right side and writing on the left. I have conversations with the images that emerge, often asking them, "Who are you?" or "What do you want me to know?" I find these journals doable, portable, and they function as diaries reflecting what is going on in my life or the larger world in fresh ways.

Collage Journal: The Point, image

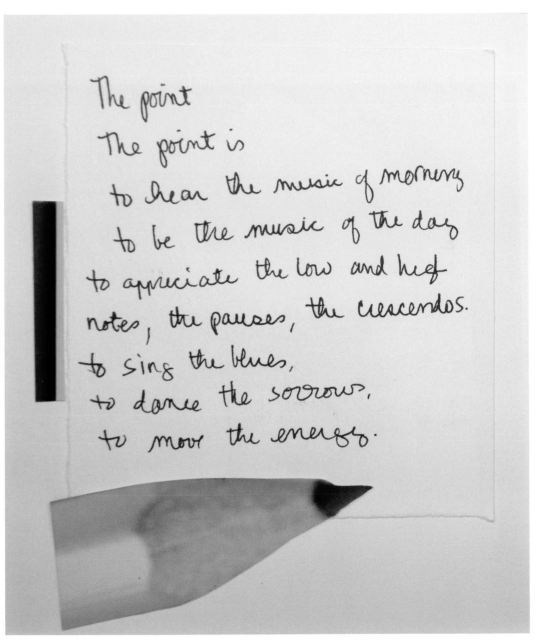

The point
The point is
to hear the music of morning
to be the music of the day
to appreciate the low and high
notes, the pauses, the crescendos.
to sing the blues,
to dance the sorrows,
to move the energy.

Collage Journal: The Point, words

This is something I can do on a regular basis to stay in touch with myself while larger projects take longer and serve me in different ways.

Collage Journal: The Color Yellow, image

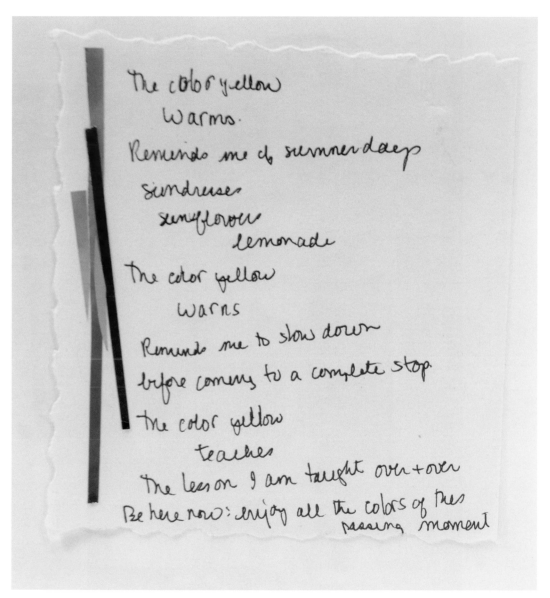

The color yellow
   Warms.
Reminds me of summer days
   Sundresses
      sunflowers
         lemonade
The color yellow
      Warns
Reminds me to slow down
before coming to a complete stop.
The color yellow
      teaches
The lesson I am taught over + over
Be here now: enjoy all the colors of this
               passing moment

Collage Journal: The Color Yellow, words

I hope you too are inspired to step into this rich world, to play freely.

My Creative Spirit

Part 2

Playing With Imagery:
My Life as Raw Material

Poems, Images, Process and Suggestions

"When words are not enough we turn to images and symbols to tell our stories. And in telling our stories through art, we find pathways to wellness, recovery and transformation."

—Cathy Malchiodi

"What lies behind us and what lies ahead of us are tiny matters compared to what lives within us."

—Henry David Thoreau

"The world is but a canvas to our imagination."

—Henry David Thoreau

Missing

Missing

Where is the child
  With wide rainbow eyes,
Apple cheeks,
Crescent moon barrettes,
In sunshine hair?

Where is the child
Afloat in the world,
A bubble bouncing,
A star beam glowing,
A dandelion dancer
With fluff-puff shoes?

Where is the child
Of wishes and wonder,
Of longing and looking,
Running and skipping.
Singing and swinging,
And playing with days?

Where is the child
Of purple and red?
Asleep? Or dead?
An adult instead?

Process Notes

As discussed in Part 1, reclaiming my playful child spirit was exactly what I needed to do to begin my healing journey through art-making. As adults we seek to control and, relying on past experience, to predict. In other words, we grown-ups view the world with presumptions and assumptions and not with the openly curious eye of the child. A child experiences excitement and amazement because everything she is discovering is new. She interacts with her immediate environment through her senses. She interprets the world by piecing together what she understands and what she is being told.

When my daughter was young, her only reference for "star" was the one atop our Christmas tree. Once she lost a balloon outside at night and was fearful that "the star's" point would prick the balloon as it drifted skyward. A poetry teacher recounts seeing her young child vigorously shaking a flowering bush in her yard. Instead of simply yelling, "Stop!" she asked the child what she was doing. The poetic reply was, "Stirring the sky."

A friend born in New York, who attended parochial school, heard the line "Lead us not into temptation" from "The Lord's Prayer" as "Lead us not into Penn Station." My children sang the John Denver song lyrics, "Sometimes I fly like an eagle, and sometimes I'm deep in despair" as "sometimes I eat the last pear."

We chuckle, but what is being demonstrated is the inner and outer play of awareness. There is an external reality, a material world of objects with which we live and move through, but our experience and understanding of that world is subjective.

I had forgotten my own active role in creating and bestowing meaning as well as how much my own imaginings colored experience. Entering the world of expressive arts was new and scary but allowed a direct experience of these powerful truths.

Mentioned before, but worth repeating, in fairy-tales the child is often offered a magic wand or an object with supernatural powers. In art making, the magic wand is the imagination. Just as the wand can make things appear or disappear, so my thoughts and beliefs have the power to create and transform outer aspects of my life.

Befriending my child self allowed me to return to that innocent originator; to be willing to experiment, to make mistakes, to abandon perfectionism. I could play in the present moment, free my imagination and return to wishing and wonder, and look upon the world with wide-eyed delight.

PLAYTIME

Some questions you might explore with art making and writing:

What awakens the child in you?

What did you love to do as a child?

What dreams did you have that you abandoned along the way: "When I grow up, I will . . ."? Does that dream still tug at your heartstrings?

Play with writing and drawing a fairy-tale with a young child as the main character. Be as spontaneous as possible, "Once upon a time . . ." Imagine the child setting out, encountering some obstacles, meeting an ally or finding some object with magical qualities. Allow the journey to unfold.

Take a walk with a young child and try to see things freshly. Allow the world to be magical and mysterious again.

Pose the question that was posed to me, "What is your worst fear?" See if you can consider it from different perspectives in order to receive new information.

I Came Seeking

I came seeking
Medicine man,
Magician,
Mystic,
Miracle worker,
Mythmaker,
Multitalented, multifaceted messiah.

I came seeking
Mother,
Mercy,
Merriment,
Moon song,
Meltdown.

Instead, I find you
Moving
Mirrors
Mirror after mirror, mirrors manifesting
Magic, mystery, miracles,
And I come to call you
Midwife,
As we labor together birthing
Myself.

Baptism

Process Notes

At the same time that I was reclaiming my child spirit, playful and agenda-free, I made another shift. I moved away from the magical thinking of the child that I still clung to, even unconsciously. While I was a responsible, middle-aged adult fulfilling the roles of wife, mother, business partner and community member, I had not completely grown up psychically. I still thought that someone or something out there held the answers for me about myself. I still thought that someone would rescue me. I still thought that others—wiser, more evolved—knew how to live this thing called life with more grace.

The poem "I Came Seeking" had originally been titled "Some M Words." On my first meeting with a therapist he asked, "Why are you here?" Considering an answer led to this poem. I was thinking, Why am I here alive, on earth? What is it I feel I am missing? What do I expect from him? As great teachers, from Socrates, ("know thyself") and his successors have maintained, the answers lie within. The work involved examining my own premises, excavating assumptions, pulling apart the pieces that composed my sense of self and my limited view of reality.

The accompanying image *Baptism* presents a figure ready to receive a blessing and a name. The ritual welcomes this new being into an ongoing group. I am taking my place in the infinity of life suggested by the hall of mirrors surrounding me.

Playtime

Some questions you might explore with art making and writing:

Have you claimed your own power?

Are you still waiting for some ideal time to begin something important to you?

How do you undermine your own intentions?

Have you decided to take responsibility for directing your own life?

You may play with images relating to birth: the idea of cycles, fertilization, incubation, gestation and delivery. What wants to birth through you?

Do a mirror process. Our face is what others see. It reveals and conceals our feelings. Take some deep breaths and then stare intently into your eyes. It's said that the eyes are the window to the soul. What wisdom from within wants to be shared? Have a conversation with yourself. Ask questions. Make a drawing of this process and journal.

Seven Soul Changes

PROCESS NOTES

As I played with images and art making, I began a deconstruction, a peeling away of layers created by conditioning, culture, training that had only resulted in confusion and illusion. I accepted my not knowing; I went back to zero, the beginning point. I began to see how all is process; everything is always in a state of becoming something else. Awareness of the moment is what matters. An important piece of the puzzle is to see the flow behind the form.

I had picked up an old sole-less shoe on a beach walk, drawn to its obvious wear and wondering about its journey. The same day I brought it home, my husband was looking at his cowboy boots, which he dearly loved and faithfully repaired. He remarked, "This one's been through seven sole changes and now it's falling apart on the inside." I wrote his words down on a piece of paper, chuckling at how they mirrored my process, and placed it inside my shoe.

Did I find this object or did it find me?

PLAYTIME

Some questions you might explore with art making and writing:

Make a point of being more attentive to what is going on around you, to objects you come across during your day, to snippets of conversation, to coincidences. You might more readily discover metaphors and symbols. I sometimes chuckle at how an event like blowing a fuse from overloading a circuit reflects my own overdoing and

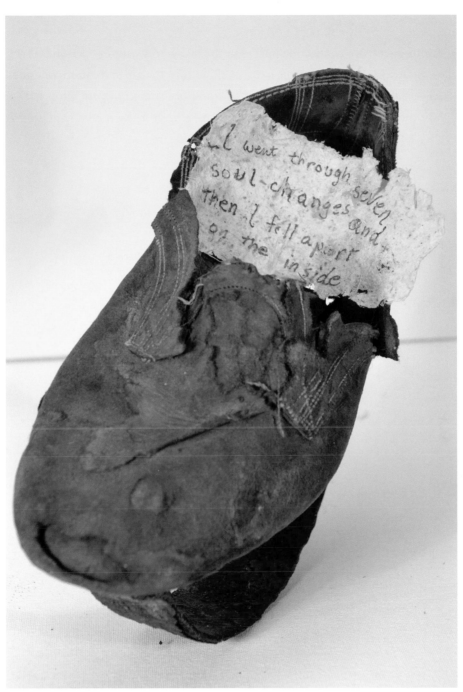

Seven Soul Changes

running out of power. Or if my washing machine stops mid-cycle because of being off balance, I am probably also out of balance.

Again, here I am connecting images in the real world with my personal process. I am allowing my inner world and the outer world to turn toward and inform one another.

Always begin by slowing down enough to notice something ordinary that sparks a suggestion of the extraordinary. Your life will open in so many ways as you do this.

Integration

Night falls
Day breaks
Humpty Dumpty falls
And breaks.
Hearts fall in love
And break.
It's a repeating pattern:
Wholeness, pieces
Whole pieces
Pieces finding their place in wholeness
Wholeness acknowledging pieces.

Reality

PROCESS NOTES

"Integration" speaks to my growing awareness that behind the surfaces are the complicated pieces making the whole. Everything alive is always changing. Nothing is static. The concepts of falling and breaking can be reframed. Leaves fall to the ground and feed the soil. I break down my food to fuel my body. My lungs expand and contract. Even my cells are always changing.

This parallels my work with collage process as I take pieces out of a whole and then make a new whole out of those pieces. I am recycling, re-visioning. This allows me to experience my life more as flow with myself as an active participant. I am beginning to accept that I am involved in creating my reality. The key is how I perceive and respond.

Life is a composting experience.

In *The Fruitful Darkness: Reconnecting with the Body of the Earth* author Joan Halifax quotes Thich Nhat Hanh:

> *The rose that wilts after six days will become a part of the garbage. After six months the garbage is transformed into a rose. When we speak of impermanence, we understand that everything is in transformation. This becomes that, and that becomes this. Looking deeply, we can contemplate one thing and see everything else in it. We are not disturbed by change when we see the interconnectedness and continuity of all things. It is not that the life of any individual is permanent, but life itself continues. When we identify ourselves with life and go beyond the boundaries of a separate identity, we shall be able to see permanence in the impermanent, or the rose in the garbage.*

The image *Reality* shows a woman staring straight ahead at the world while her head bursts with images behind her eyes, including a bird perched on a branch. Ideas flitter in my brain, sometimes resting momentarily, sometimes taking up residency.

PLAYTIME

Some questions you might explore with art making and writing:

Think back to the many transformations you have been through: baby to toddler, child to adult. Remember how each stage morphs into the next. Focus on the ever-widening orbits of experience.

Were transitions hard? Were you excited and/or scared to enter a new phase?

Recall some events in your life that held both elements: an ending and a beginning. Write or perform an art process around some aspects of that change.

Write a poem honoring what has passed, recognizing what might have created space for what came next.

Create a fairy-tale about a journey: yours, someone's close to you, or that of someone imagined.

Explore how you create your own reality. Recall a time when a situation was misinterpreted, either by you or by someone else. How can we keep our perspective clear and unclouded?

Pedestal

I took an ax
And whacked
The leg off the pedestal
You had me on.
And then I whacked
The leg off the pedestal
I had you on.
And with the hacked-off pieces,
I built a bridge,
For you to walk over to me,
And me to walk over to you,
On our very own,
Very human, legs

My Angels Walk on Earth

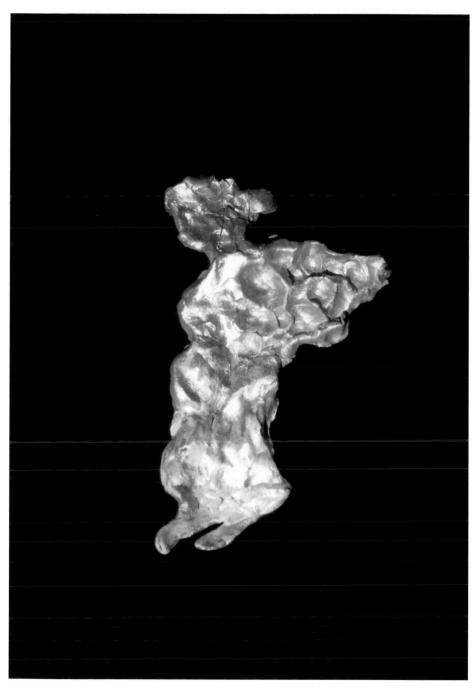

Rabbit-Footed Angel

PROCESS NOTES

"Pedestal" reflects my growing awareness and acceptance that I am a flawed human being and that my flaws make me more human. This is true for each of us. Once again, there is a deconstruction process occurring here, resulting in pieces that can then be re-purposed to build something new. Empowering myself means moving out of my head, taking action in the real world.

The image *My Angels Walk on Earth* is one of the very first that I made. Here is my child self, recognizing I am now all grown up and grounded on earth. The shoes are a cut-up photo of the earth. The adult is a man suggesting I need to own my own power.

I also add a clay figure, *Rabbit-Footed Angel*. Here, again, the image instructs. This angel has very large feet, suggesting a rabbit to me. Rabbits have the ability to jump high, leaping because their strong feet use the ground as a springboard. I need to ground my expectations and live my desires.

PLAYTIME

Some questions you might explore with art making and writing:

Consider whom you have placed on a pedestal. And who do you think has placed you on one?

What are the qualities you project onto others? Can you recognize these qualities in yourself?

Make a drawing that expresses something about how it feels to come down to earth. Or how it feels to be revered. Write about the process.

Petit Pas

I sought wings
Felt buds ripening on my back
Caressed their tight knots.
Found feathers on the ground and treated each
As treasure
Symbols of my special kinship with angels.
I opened doors on metal cages—
Including the protective mesh around my heart—
Let ornamental birds and wooden angels
Fly free.

Later, much later
After my wings were weary with circling
I looked at the cages and knew spirit
Can spring through bars
There is no holding back except by self
Too fearful to fly.
My wings let me see that I could choose
That I also needed
Feet.

Shrine to Foot

Process Notes

"Petit Pas" (Little Steps) continues the theme of finding my feet, so I made a plaster cast of my actual foot. I placed dried petals and rosebuds around it. I see this as an honoring, a shrine. I added the tissue parasols as a celebratory touch. I have found that my feet are agents of movement. I am an expressive, active participant in the dance of life. The hollowness within is not emptiness but a vessel for my spirit. Much of my work was coming home to my body rather than living in my mind. The foot is most important as it grounds me to the earth. I am bridging spirit with matter, embodying my soul.

PLAYTIME

Some questions you might explore with art making and writing:

Think about feet. The phrases, metaphors and idioms are abundant: the next step, putting the right foot forward, place one foot after the other, walk your talk, walk a mile in someone's shoes.

Think about shoes. They reflect roles and activities: sneakers, sports; slippers, indoors; work shoes, task-focused; boots, outdoors, or cowboys; heels, dressing up; sandals summer. Viewing your collection of shoes, do you feel a balance of work/play? Play with designing a shoe for a part of you that wants more attention: maybe a sequined dance slipper or a super energizer running shoe.

Are your shoes paired or is one missing?

Create a story about shoes off on an adventure. Perhaps the shoes are magical and have special powers? Let your imagination go. Illustrate and write the story.

The Invisible World

I close
My eyes to see,
Within
Is the screen
Upon which all
Without
Is projected.
How can we even agree
On the color green?

With our hands
We might near
A common understanding.
If we stretch
Them before us
Over a candle
Flame we might
Both feel
The warmth
       And touch.

The Invisible World

PROCESS NOTES

The poem "The Invisible World" relates to my growing awareness that each of us creates a reality with our mind that might not always be accurate. I may project motives or make assumptions that create problems for myself. Each of us sees through our own eyes and from a distinct perspective. In a way, we are writing a novel with the stories we tell ourselves. There really is no possible way of truly connecting with others unless we are willing to recognize these filters.

To bridge the separation also requires letting go of being right. My mother, who suffered from dementia, lived with us. We could be having a discussion or argument and she would be confused. I *knew* I was right but being right became irrelevant in speaking with her. Establishing a warm connection was the important thing.

The image *The Invisible World* conveys the insubstantial nature of reality and honors the spiritual dimension, the unseen. "What is essential is invisible to the eye. It is only with the heart that one can truly see," as Antoine de Saint-Exupéry had his Little Prince say.

PLAYTIME

Some questions you might explore with art making and writing:

Compose a drawing or collage of your heart, a heart with eyes. Or make a three-dimensional piece. What does your heart see?

Create a mask. You can purchase premade mask forms in a variety of materials. Make the front the "seen," what you show others, and the back, the "unseen," your inner world.

Consider all the processes going on within your body and in nature that are invisible but vitally important.

Reflect on this process through writing.

Seeing

The 49ers cap, his red roof
   The Cubs striped jersey, his wall.
The boy within his house.
The man within the boy.
At twelve, they battle for tenancy.
The boy has squatter's rights
The man, powerful hormones.
Sometimes I peer into his eyes
His windows
For clues
Who is home today?
I see a soul peering back
Neither boy nor man
Seeing me
Neither mom nor woman.

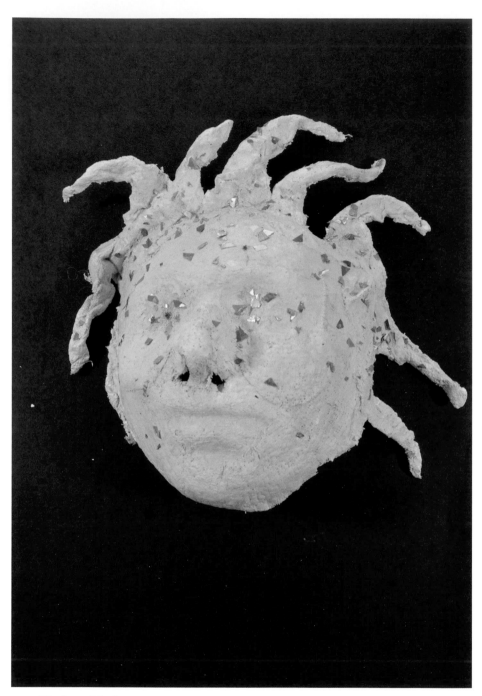

Trickster Mask

PROCESS NOTES

My son at twelve was sometimes a cuddly kid, sometimes a challenging adolescent. "Seeing" allowed me to move beyond the battleground that puberty can create for families. A momentary awareness hit me that both my son and I were souls on a journey. We needed help to navigate these rough seas of adolescence. This awareness was that help. Now I could step back in the midst of some exchange and allow some space. I am grateful that the writing held the flash of insight, and that I heard that whisper and gave it volume.

This mask is a cast of my own head. I have added bits of glitter to suggest magic and a jester hat to suggest trickery. My eyes do play tricks on me, and seeing is a magical act.

Best Poem

The best poem ever is four words:
Good-bye. I love you.
These four words
My daughter utters over and over.
At bedtime, school time, any parting time.
"Good-bye. I love you."
She speaks these four words
Heavy with the weight
Of centuries of partings
Heavy with the tears
And sorrows of countless separations
Tosses them lightly behind her
Sometimes like petals
More often like crumbs dropped.

She seems to need to speak them.
As a rosary? As a mantra?
As a finger-crossing?
An inner prompting
Planted when?
An irresistible command
Whose voice?
Makes her mouth the words.

After yelling, "I hate you!
I hate Alex! I hate, hate . . ."
She clenches her teeth
Grabs her pack
Rushes out.
Almost makes it.
But before slamming the door
Sticks her head back in
Knowing she can't escape
The pressing necessity
Even
In the midst of rage
Especially
In the midst of rage,
"Good-bye. I love you."
She speaks these four words.

I hear her speaking them for all of us,
Who held our tongues
Over and over
Or missed the chance altogether.

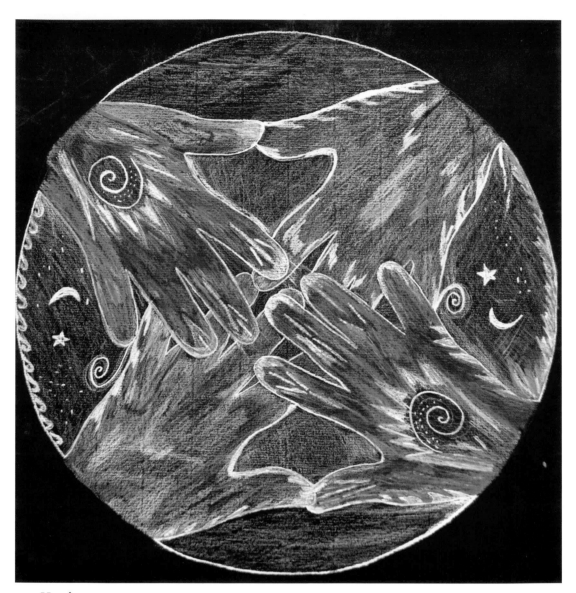

Hands

PROCESS NOTES

"Best Poem" connects me to the larger soul in my daughter. This ritualized parting caught my attention especially as I was experiencing loss in my own life that didn't easily allow these good-byes. I was struck by her commitment to saying these words whenever she left.

This image shows hands reaching across time, touching or waving. Our paths intersect with others in mysterious ways.

My process of self-reflection served my family as these two poems illustrate. I could own my own needs and perceptions, sharing them as honestly as possible. Expanding my own sense of self extended to others as well.

PLAYTIME

Some questions you might explore with art making and writing:

Can you broaden the lens with which you see those closest to you? Change perspectives, zoom in, or zoom out?

Create a play, either a comedy or drama, with your family or circle of friends as the cast.

Place someone in a new context or switch the roles, positioning your child as your parent for example, and create a dialogue. Be as spontaneous as possible.

Draw or collage any of these options.

Notions on Motions

Basketball in Boonville
Ballet in Cotton
Beginning and ending of a Saturday
Alex's first game: a thriller, overtime victory.
Bodies bounding and bouncing
Floorboards and scoreboards sounding
Thump-thump, jungle sounds
Buzz-buzz, jingle bells.

The dancers bound and bounce, too
Drum the floor
Bring the life out from within
They are liquid
Honey flowing sensually into shapes
Illusions of something solid
They are neon gas
Energy throbbing into form
They are moonlight
Allowing feelings to be seen.

And I, an audience to both game and dance
Watching athletes alive in their bodies
Artists in step with their vision
Feel invited
To move.

Taking Flight

Blue Moon Fantasy

Bronze dancer
Frozen form: perfect, poised, controlled.
In the golden garden
Becomes unhinged
Loses head
Heart takes flight.

On a blue moon night
    Bronze melts to honey
        Flows into delight.

Blue Moon Fantasy

PROCESS NOTES

"Notions on Motions" captures a day in our lives that began while we watched our son's basketball game in a nearby town and ended at a ballet performance in an auditorium. Both activities demonstrated the vitality and beauty of energized bodies. Following my own impulses, giving my spirit wings and feet, is important. To be fully alive I must connect the spiritual to the physical plane.

I explored the freedom of dance further in the collage *Taking Flight*. I experience being invited to become the *dance*. I don't have to wait for someone to teach me the steps. I only have to move my feet to discover my wings.

"Blue Moon Fantasy" is also about moving from rigidity to fluidity. I found the image of Degas's bronze statue, *Little Dancer*. I felt she was frozen, confined by a disciplined pose. Her fabric tutu— soft, flimsy and transparent—was a stark contrast to the hard metal. I wanted the heart to open like a hinge to let the spirit fly. The poem followed the collage. Honey and bees are creeping more and more into my imagery.

PLAYTIME

Some questions you might explore with art making and writing:

Do you feel frozen or stuck in any areas of your life? Put on some music, close your eyes and let your body begin to sway and perhaps dance.

After doing some exercise, even just walking, draw a line to depict your energy before and after. Do some free scribbles to loosen up.

Play with a young toddler.

Fusion

There is in me a hollow
A holy hole
Like that burnt-out base in the ancient redwood tree
That beckoned us that day
An opening to heaven
Where fire burns from time to time
Bright orange flames
Rising up from base
Through core
Creating flaming golden crown
Ablaze I am
Consumed in origins
Birthing universes
All light can fill my holy hole
Expanded with heat
Immense with life
There is in me a hollow
A holy hole.

Embody

Enchantment

Process Notes

Connecting my spirituality and my sexuality was an important step in my becoming whole. The body is the soul's home and must be honored. Our culture does not make this easy. Religion can create a split, some even with creation stories depicting our fall from grace. Some teach that our bodies and desires are shameful and our flesh is to be punished. Media sensationalizes and cheapens desire. Learning to love and appreciate my body and to receive and offer pleasure is quite a challenge.

The collage *Embody* depicts my humanness. I want to accept my sensuality and the vulnerability that implies. I am a teapot, pouring out. I am alive and fluid.

Enchantment shows a woman with a winged body dancing, She has been awakened to the enchantments of life, called by the music of life to take flight.

Playtime

Some questions you might explore with art making and writing:

Reflect on what feeds your senses. What experiences give you pleasure?

Sitting by a fire, watching the sun set or rise, walking in a forest, to a waterfall, or on the beach?

Listening to music? Dancing? Playing sports/running?

Cooking? Dining? Sex?

Do you allow yourself to savor what delights you?

Do you struggle with deserving, denying yourself something because you haven't "earned" it?

American Airlines

"American Airlines announces the arrival of Flight 177 from New York. You may meet passengers at Gate 63."

I stand behind the glass as the plane
A swollen red, white and blue fish docks.
A small square net, ridiculously out of proportion
Looms ready to catch the rainbow fish.
Instead it meets the glass of cockpit
A kiss to signal home.
My brother has tennis balls suspended in his garage
For precision parking, too.
I watch as the tunnel arm connects
As toy-sized pilots write on clipboards
As ear-muffed parka-clad workers
Bustle with wood blocks, tractors and wagons.
I see you as a toddler on your knees
Powering planes with your hands
Along carpet, into air, down again
To dart under chair legs.
I see you plucking plug-like people
With bald plastic heads
From the plane's underbelly.
You walk these stubby people
Over cushions, tables, back onto the plane.

You whisk the plane from floor to air
With high arcs and spins.
Always it lands
You, the omnipotent pilot
A hand outside
Holding everything.

I stand behind the glass
Like a new parent at the nursery window
Overcome with what is to come.
This red, white and blue plane
Like a beached whale
Lurching into stillness
Has been places I've never been
Now returns you
My 15-year-old firstborn.
You've been where I've not been
This trip, the first.
My hand no longer holding yours
Waved good-bye.
Now I'm behind glass
Holding space within my heart
Practicing faith like a novice nun
The practice itself, the faith.

I watch as passengers
Stroll free of the elbow-shaped tunnel
Into arms of human connectors.
I overhear snippets of greetings.
A toddler's cry, "Daddy, Daddy!"
My expectations run into theirs
Same questions

Each passenger different and yet the same.
More and more pass me by
The stream of people runs dry.

The fear I set aside
When I let you go
Begins to pulse
It always lies at the ready
Needing only my halting breath
To breathe itself alive
Instantly huge.
My mind quiets the fear
Asks it to be still.
I need to be ready for whatever is next.
Just as I accept the possibility—
You, I see.

You, lugging bags, boxes, poster tube
Slightly off balance
A shy smile trying to break free
Of your cool, worldly pose.

You tell me you almost
Missed your flight
You ran to enter closing doors
You tell me you would have had to fly to Chicago
Had a six-hour layover
You tell me I would have been mad
Meeting you at three in the morning.
You tell me you saw three freeway crashes
Traffic terrible in New York
The words flood out.

I am overcome with relief.
I, we, escaped all these near misses
All these accidents
All the dangers lurking
In this big and beautiful world.
We walk and talk
Through the terminal
Amid so many possibilities
On the move once more
After a moment of stillness
Two stubby people
In the hands of someone
Or something
Holding
Everything.

Yellow Bird

PROCESS NOTES

Our children leave the safe haven of our homes and arms to journey farther afield, starting at kindergarten or before. Their orbits continue to expand. Learning to trust, letting go, and to instill confidence in them is our job. Still, when my son took his first flight to New York alone as a young teenager, I found myself excited and terrified. I was so happy to meet him at the airport on his return. This poem conveys that experience.

The collage *Yellow Bird* is from one of my small journals. I select it to depict my young son flying off on his own, leaving the nest.

PLAYTIME

Some questions you might explore with art making and writing:

Create a collage shield to offer protection for your loved ones. What do you want to provide them with for a safe journey through life? Find imagery to represent the qualities that you decide on.

Make a small pouch as a container for words of support and inspiration that you have selected.

What do you want to pass on? You can also do this as a box project, or a suitcase. Imagine packing good luck charms and talismans.

Create an object that holds your love, perhaps a doll with wooden clothes-pegs or popsicle sticks decorated with fabric, ribbons, feathers.

For self-comfort create small "worry" dolls then place them in a representation of safety. I light candles by photos.

The Home Chord or Saying Goodnight to Kate

Tonight
        Putting you to bed
Back of my hand
To your temples
Stroking your face
Slow, worshipful caresses,
I time travel.

Beneath my fingers
I feel you newborn
My fingers touching
First touch
Your skin, YOUR skin,
Cell to cell.
    (Oh, how long we touched
      Cell to cell, my inside to your outside,
      You growing inside my inside.)
Still, this moment coming together,
Face to face, skin to skin
Feels
First touch
Cell to cell
Speaking through fingertips

Signing sacred words:
"I love you."
"I wonder at you."
"I welcome you."

My tears running
Baptizing your moist head
Nestled beneath my chin.

I caress creases of newborn skin
Wrinkles everywhere:
Neck, inside elbows, wrists
Thighs, knees, toes, fingers.
I gently knead your dimpled hands,
Like rippled ponds
Caress
In unspeakable gratitude
For your perfection.

My lips follow paths of fingertips
Kissing your forehead
Pale, pale eyebrow arch
Nose tip, cheek, shoulder
Each crease, each toe, each finger.
Like a dog licking her pup
I mark you as mine.

Tonight,
You, nearly ten, lie beneath a canopy
Your head full of dreams
A light burning for nightmares.
You ask for a cuddle

I oblige
Stretch out by your side.
You have grown into your skin
Grown to almost my size.
I stroke your face
Back of my hand to your temples
Slow, worshipful caresses.

You chatter
My fingers pass
The wrinkle-free corner of your eye
I see the time when I won't be here.

Time when old woman
Replaces young girl
Inside and out
When your face, this face
Shows the traces
Of dreams and nightmares
When form begins to shrink
Skin loosens again
As body moves homeward.

I feel beneath my fingers
Your wrinkled, fuzzy skin
Not as newborn but as
New crone.

I put my mother's face on yours.
I stroke more gently
As if you were her.
        (Last summer

Didn't I nestle her
Beneath my chin
In bear hug
Pat-patting
Holding
Simply holding her
Like a newborn
Needing comfort
As her tears flowed?)

You are her.
I am her.
She is me.
I am you.
You are me.
We are all in this dance.
Lover and beloved.

I stroke your fingers.
Smile . . .
At your neck arching back.
I have seen that same pose
Created while floating
Within my belly
As you fell asleep on my breast
On crib pillow
Now in canopy bed
Later on lover's chest
In rocking chair nap
In satin creases
Within coffin's womb.

I catch my tears
In your golden hair
Snuggle close
My silver hair falls
 to weave with yours.

I caress you
    In unspeakable gratitude
        For the perfection of this love.

Mother's Arms

Process Notes

While studying piano as an adult beginner, I thought chords were magical. I was fascinated by how three notes together created this amazing sound. The home chord consists of middle C, E and G. I made the connection to the three generations of my family: my mother, myself and my daughter. I saw us as three individuals tied together through the umbilical cord. I was exploring the concepts of joining and separating, insides and outsides, growing outward and inward, growing up and growing old. My mother was dealing with dementia and often felt like my baby. Once, bathing and dressing her reminded me of playing with dolls as a kid. Her vulnerability evoked such tenderness. On the other end of the cycle was my young daughter, about to leave the innocence of childhood. I was acutely aware of the preciousness of life.

"The Home Chord" relates a flash of insight triggered by a simple gesture, saying goodnight; a magic moment tying all these thoughts together.

The collage *Mother's Arms* shows a daughter in her mother's arms while the mother is held in the universal arms of Mother Nature. The tree branches embrace and the adult face loses its features, blurring into eternity.

Playtime

Some questions you might explore with art making and writing:

Create an altar to your ancestors, including significant others who influenced your life. Place photos and objects that had meaning in their lives, adding anything you feel you need to complete the altar.

Write a letter thanking each person. Write a letter to your children.

The Runaway Word

The runaway word was "perfect"
Upside down on the floor,
Safe, forever out of reach

Or

The word "perfect"
Ran away
Hid upside down on the carpet
Forever impossible to find.

Giving Myself a Black "I" or Kicking Myself in the "I"

PROCESS NOTES

Before I was certified as an art therapist I worked as a counselor at the local schools. While there, I often worked with self-esteem issues and as a sort of Mr. Rogers, reassuring the students that "you are perfect just the way you are." But perfection was the villain. "The Runaway Word" followed a time when we were playing with my magnetic poetry board.

Unrealistic expectations and standards of perfection plague adolescents. They compare themselves to others and judge themselves extremely harshly. Witnessing their conflicts with others and with themselves confirmed the lessons I was learning. For as adults we continue this undermining process.

Giving Myself a Black "I" or Kicking Myself in the "I" echos this theme of self-loathing. Feeling locked in and uptight, I am a prisoner (convict stripes) of my emotions. When I am envious, resentful, spiteful, I'm a victim. My body is hot with the heat of my emotions, and my head is exploding with fiery damaging thoughts. Teenagers can be their own worst enemies. I wanted to make them aware of how we hurt ourselves with our negative thoughts and help them discover new messages that strengthen their self-image.

PLAYTIME

Some questions you might explore with art making and writing:

Do you struggle with perfection? One of the earliest art experiences I had was being asked to paint a truly ugly picture. I chose colors I didn't like and just smeared away. There is something to be said for abandoning the effort to be perfect or do our best. Give yourself total permission to let loose. This is true play.

Make a nest or container of some sort to house your need for perfection. Maybe place eggshells in there to symbolize walking on eggs. Think of other traps that perfection places in your way. How many projects are never completed or perhaps never even started because perfection raises its head? Draw that head.

Return

Leaving the main road,
Entering the twisted path,
Slowing down,
Slowing way down,
I park,
 Move into the dark
Small among towering trees.
I step on stones
Each one leads me
Closer to the door
With its scribed instruction.
I enter
The sacred circle,
I enter
My sacred center.
From here we share
Our deepest selves,
Allowing, inviting, celebrating.
Trust intimacy is possible,
Blessing the dark, the light,
The movement, the pauses,
The space between, as the space within.

Harlequin About Faces/Mystery

From Where I Am

From where I am
I receive
Am entered into and give
From where I am.
I am not where someone else is
In this moment
This sliver of enchantment.
Yet I know in my body/heart/spirit
Where they are
Because we are here together.
I sense the connection
From where I am.

From where I am
I hold where I have been
Where they are.
I am not anything less
Because they are more.
I am where I am.
Like the moon, I wax and wane.
All I have to do is honor
Where I am
Listen to my heart
Be a part
Be where I am
From where I am.

In My Own Hands

Life, the Universe and Everything

The Art *of* Play

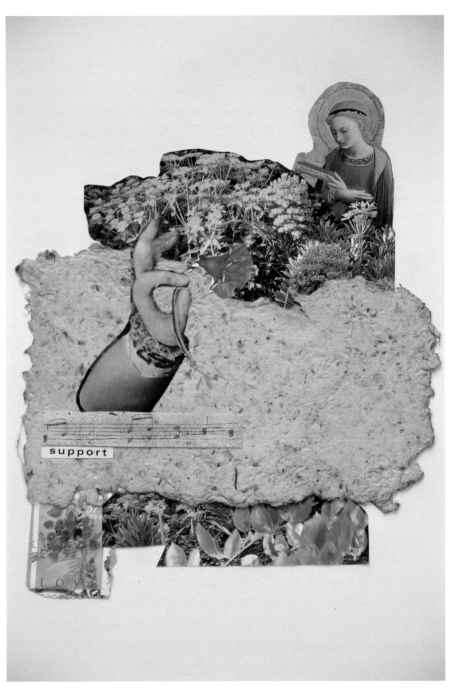

Support

Process Notes

I once belonged to a group that met regularly to share our creative process, be it music, writing or art. The leader created safety by having us respond with personal responses after someone shared something. We were not to judge or critique but to say how we were affected by their piece, what we experienced, what associations arose, etc. These poems are about those evenings.

The first, "Return," conveys the sense of entering an altered space. This is what I try to create when I engage with my own creative process. One of the chief benefits of doing creative work communally is that we discover how we are alike in so many ways, despite surface differences. We recognize ourselves in each other, and we see our roles in a much larger story. When I allow another's story or image to enter me and I respond with imagery as if it were my own, I am able to experience things I would never feel in my own life. My heart opens. I connect to our human condition more intimately. Compassion is possible.

The collage *Harlequin About Faces/Mystery* rests on an Escher background that transforms concepts of figure/ground as well as the figures within that field. Chessmen are upside down; birds morph into blocks. Reality is many layered. Like a jester, Harlequin confuses and amuses. He tricks our perceptions, invites us into a liminal space where things shift and emerge. A wise fool, shamanistic, he leads us into the transpersonal realm. This is how I experience the art group. Wondrous things happen. While we are safe in our little nest, we journey together, exploring mystery.

"From Where I Am" addresses this experiment in authentic communication with one another. The idea was to be fully who we were each evening. We had complete permission to bring all parts of ourselves to the table. The shadow was always a welcome guest as pretending or denying traps energy better used to create!

The collage *In My Own Hands* explores the Great Mystery, the magic act of time: now you see it, now you don't; here and gone. I photocopied my hands and placed them on a stage. On the stage of life, my very own hands have the ability and responsibility to create; to tap the egg and reveal the life within.

The collage *Life, the Universe and Everything* continues the theme of time, impermanence and my small but significant part to play in life unfolding. Again I place a hand this time holding a nest bearing a single egg. What will be born? Our group feels like this sacred garden space.

The collage *Support* recognizes the group as my support system. It is a fertile space filled with love.

PLAYTIME

Some questions you might explore with art making and writing:

Consider your relationship to mystery. Make a drawing to express something about that.

Create an altar to mystery.

Recognize where you find and who offers you support for expressing your true most authentic self, your uniqueness. Write a letter thanking them. Make a drawing that represents how that support feels and place it where it can continue to serve you.

Represent your creative spirit with a drawing, a collage, a doll or totem.

Create an altar honoring your creativity.

Of course, I recommend joining a creative art group.

The Singer

She rises from her place in the circle,
Holding tears and vulnerability tonight.
Moves to the bench
Lifts her hands, breathes
Empties to receive,
To meet the piano before her.
Lover, friend, teacher.
Her fingers touch down
The melody rises
A veil drawn
Revealing
Tender longing
Clear wisdom
A lullaby to awaken
Strong passion
Her voice
As gentle as a breeze
Mighty as a tornado.

The Singer

PROCESS NOTES

"The Singer" is my response to another's time at the piano. I so envied this woman's talent. Then I realized that she offered us a gift and our job was to receive it with gratitude. The music she created with her voice and the piano took us on a journey, allowing us to feel our own feelings more deeply.

The collage *The Singer* shows the transporting quality of music.

Show Your Colors

PROCESS NOTES

The collage *Show Your Colors* is about not hiding. The peacock proudly displays his colors but is judged as vain. Many of us are conditioned to *inhibit* instead of *inhabit* our exuberance. As I play with art I am invited to express freely and fully. I recall a card stating, "What is not given is lost." The expressive art process is about flowering not cowering. The following quote from *A Return to Love* by Marianne Williamson reinforces this premise:

"Our greatest fear is not that we are inadequate. Our deepest fear is that we are powerful beyond measure. It is our light not our darkness that most frightens us. Who am I to be brilliant, gorgeous, talented and fabulous. Actually who are you not to be. You are a child of God. Your playing small doesn't serve the world. There is nothing enlightened about shrinking so that other people won't feel insecure around you. We were born to make manifest the glory of God within us. It is not just in some of us it is in everyone and as we let our own light shine we unconsciously give others permission to do the same. As we are liberated from our own fears our presence automatically liberates others."

PLAYTIME

Some questions you might explore with art making and writing:

Do you suffer from "Compare-ment impairment," a term I coined to represent the dangers of comparing ourselves to others?

It is very hard to recover from this handicap but not impossible. The best cure is reminding yourself to have fun, to play. With art, it is OK to copy another or borrow an idea or technique. You will create something original. Find something that inspires you and go ahead and try to replicate it.

Playing with children is highly recommended.

Empty Nest/Nest Wanting Wings

I am a nest no longer needed,
A depression in my center
Where new life once lived.
First encased in delicate shell,
Eggs resting on my downy inside,
Padded with fur, feather, fuzz,
A cushion against woven twigs,
Sharp edges.
Then as hatchlings,
Ravenous, gawky bodies with open beaks.
Later as young birds,
Beautiful beings, discovering wings.
I am high, my perch a tree elbow.
Isolated for safety, hidden from predators,
Camouflaged.
Strong to withstand winds.

I have been incubator, protector,
Landing site and departure gate.
I have been of use.
Now I am a nest no longer needed.
Not empty, for I hold in this hollow place,
All that has been;

I am a restless nest,
No longer content with holding and being held.

Could these bits of broken shell,
Like seeds that know to grow, to become
Hold the secret of my flight?

Nest Wanting Wings

PROCESS NOTES

This poem was written as a group exercise at a conference workshop following the prompt, "Pick any object and write from the 'I am' place." We were to look around the room, our desks, or out the window for stimulation. I first wrote about being a cannonball as there was a cannon on the grounds. Then I saw the nest and this came.

"Empty Nest/Nest Wanting Wings" is about change, the one constant in life. As my children fly off into their futures, who or what still wants to live through me?

The drawing is self-explanatory.

PLAYTIME

Some questions you might explore with art making and writing:

Do this same exercise of finding any object and writing from the "I am" place. Stick with the attributes of the object as much as possible and be spontaneous.

Or, following the theme of my poem, what still wants to be birthed through you?

Have you put aside something important that you wanted to do, due to your busy life?

Think of that as a seed growing in darkness, germinating, awaiting your attention to grow into the light.

Recall different transitions in your life, remembering the awkward liminal phase where the new is not quite formed and you may not be quite finished with the old. Think of twilight, a blending, a shifting of day to night. And think of dawn. Make a drawing to express something about that.

Paprika Seasonings on Summer Greens

Summer's "forever"
Falls
Away,
Drops like overripe apples
Onto crisp leaves.
Rust replaces
Spring's bright reds;
Daffodils' yellows
Burn to gold.
Piles of raked leaves
Become smoke,
Disappear,
Buds to ashes.

At fifty-two, I love this time
Of fading/brightening
Even more.
Shadows lengthen, my palette grows,
As days shorten.

I would not trade *this* fall
For fifty-two springs,
And yet,
I cannot stop my tears.

Rust

PROCESS NOTES

Of course aging is the big change that requires my appreciation as well as acceptance. As I more fully recognize my own mortality, I receive the passing moments as gifts. I am aware of the richness of life as well as its sorrows. "Paprika Seasonings on Summer's Greens" captures this recognition and acceptance of both states. I am no longer maiden, but crone holding much in my heart. I have a deeper appreciation for life and greater compassion because of having lived through experiences that open my heart.

The collage *Rust* seems perfect here: ripe oranges on a platter, rusty leaves falling down.

PLAYTIME

Some questions you might explore with art making and writing:

Think of associations with the autumn season. It is a time of harvesting.

As you reflect on your life, what lessons have you learned?

What can you "preserve" to see you through the winter to come?

The fall equinox offers an opportunity to consider balance in our lives. Create a pie with sections to represent the different roles and responsibilities that occupy your time. Does this feel balanced?

The nights grow longer. How do you feel about darkness? Do you dream?

How do you feel about the shift from the more active, outer energy of summer to the quieter, internal energy of winter?

Express some of these reflections.

On Turning Six-"O"

Part of the river flowing
    Part of the ancient migration
On the road winding ever forward
From birth to death
And perhaps beyond
Or circling back.
Part of the building up and tearing down
In the moment
In the eternal
At six-"o" I dance
The dance of life
Tossing the zero like a ball
Shaping the "o" like an exclamation
The point being
To gather rosebuds all along the way
To savor the passing
To welcome what's next
Shaping that "o" like a prayer
Of gratitude and faith.

Turning 60

PROCESS NOTES

On my sixtieth birthday, I reflect on lessons learned. As I grow older I am ever more aware of how quickly time passes, of what grows in significance, and of what fades—becoming unimportant. There is a freedom from earlier concerns and a freedom to be more myself.

The collage is a portrayal of time flowing, of journeying and of playing at being OK with it all.

PLAYTIME

Some questions you might explore with art making and writing:

Draw the story of your life. Perhaps collage it on a map background.

Create a small book with chapters for different ages; for example toddlerhood, childhood, the teen years, adulthood, senior years—depending on your age. You can make little pouches with envelopes to hold photos or images of memories or any material that holds significance for you. Different eras will have different energies, which you can represent with colors or symbols. Allow some un-actualized dreams to enter and see if any want to be realized at this point.

Draw your life as a fairy-tale or mythic journey.

What matters most in your life right now?

What do you like most about being your current age?

Part One: Painted Face

The makeup on her face is painted by life.
The lines are story lines.
They tell of the many lives she's touched,
The many lives that have touched her.
Living leaves impressions
These lines mark where contact is made.
Her wrinkled skin speaks volumes
These lines here, the traces of smiles,
Those lines there, the furrows of frowns
Here below the eye,
A canal carved by tears.
Her eyes see clearly both visible and invisible worlds
She has night vision
Is familiar with shapes shifting
The known into the unknown
The unknown into the known
She walks in the dark forest at night
A golden globe for a flashlight
She smiles the smile of the very wise
The clown, the seductress, the saint
Does she clarify or distort with her mirror
Reflecting ages of lines
Infinite story lines
I only know as I walk one step at a time to meet her
We each walk alone

Along this path of the many.
Facing her face, seeing my face etched on her skin
Her face becoming mine
I ask, "What do I need to know first?
What do I need to know last?
What can you who have walked ahead, tell me
Of this path, my path, our path?"

Her eyes blue deep pools
Stare straight through me
Reflect only eyes looking
Her red lipstick smile
Painted as on a mannequin
As inscrutable as a pasty Oriental mask
Says silently.
"Listen for the unsaid."

We part.
I turn, walk back to the daylight world
She simply disappears
into tree bark, branch
And the moonlit sky.

Part Two: Forest-Wise Woman

At first I take her for tree
Her outstretched hand a branch
Moving with the night wind
Then I see her eyes
Clear, blue pools
Her glowing white, lined face
Her silvery hair.

She stands tall
Tall, like the trees around her
Who hold her in their arms
Her cloak flows loose
Woven of leaf, moss, bark.
Her smile is radiant
She holds a mirror in one hand
A globe in the other.

I am attracted and yet
Afraid to move toward her
To touch her outstretched hand
Wisps of spider webs silky and sticky
Surround her as she moves
Slowly, steadily
To meet me.

I remember the tale of Spider Grandmother
The myth of Arachne
I feel my blood pulsing
Each pore alive and sensing
Her smile reminds
This walk of mine
Is a blink of an eye.

She Reaches Out

Part Three: Forest Crone

I walk in dark woods
She appears, walking toward me
At first I take her for a tree branch
Moving with the wind
Her hair mossy, leafy
Her skin like bark
Her lips, wine red
Her eyes
Blue pools
She is at home in this world of
Shiftings and sheddings
She says nothing with words
Simply reassures
That nature is home
To everything there is a season
The little girl skipping with light step
Lives inside this gnarled frame
As does the beautiful young woman
And she
The older, wiser one of silence
Lived waiting inside them.

The Crone (assemblage)

Process Notes

"Meeting the Crone" was written after a guided visualization. I did several images to deepen the experience. I felt my face aging and saw the lines that time created as story lines. The collage "She Reaches Out" attempts to portray the imagery I encountered on my imaginal journey. The assemblage was the final representation for me. I am facing my own death, the great mystery of life and death. I hold within me all my former ages like Russian nesting dolls. I add an empty nest with an eggshell at the top left; a raven representing death and change, top right; a nest with an intact egg, lower left, along with a photo of Alice Liddell, the girl who inspired *Alice in Wonderland.* The crone face itself is a basket inverted and covered with tissue paper, moss, fur and seeds.

Playtime

Some questions you might explore with art making and writing:

Make your own representation of the crone archetype.

Have an older "you" write a letter to the present "you" sharing wisdom gained over time. Tuck this away somewhere.

What are your fears about aging?

What are gifts that come with aging?

Death by Honey

Today I lift the lid of honey pot
And see the ant corpses
Black bodies drowned in gold
Not 30 million-year-old dinosaur DNA
Embedded miraculously in amber
But hungry hunters
Here, at last
After marching miles
Searching
At their goal.

Sweet treat, sweet death.
Did they taste
As they were swallowed
By their meal?

I suppose of the many deaths
Death by honey is not so bad.

Today I wrapped the old cat Stormy
In towels and love
Drove her on her last ride.
Teary-eyed
Knowing it was mercy
To send this worn-out body to rest.

A friend seeks to comfort and says,
"Remember what the Indians said,
'Do not worry about what you do,
Worry about what you waste.'"

I'm not sure I understand.

Of loving and losing and endings
I know even less.

Golden Pear

PROCESS NOTES

One morning while making tea, I opened the lid on the honey pot to see many ant corpses. Whenever I see an errant ant on my counter I think of their colonies, their industry, their commitment to scout out whatever they need. I feel guilty killing them and often transport them outdoors. They sometimes arrive on cut flowers and I imagine their displacement. This particular day I was going to take our old cat to the vet to be put to sleep. I thought of seeking, about endings of long journeys, our ultimate destination of death. We had recently seen the film *Jurassic Park*, in which amber preserves potential life from ancient times. All these pieces came together. I am aware of mystery, of living, dying, connecting—and losing.

This collage, *Golden Pear*, is still a mystery piece for me. I haven't any story. I selected images and colors that pleased me and added textures. I found it comforting, so chose it to be with this poem about Stormy.

PLAYTIME

Some questions you might explore with art making and writing:

Writing and art making can serve as a container for the intense feelings that follow the loss or death of loved ones. Simply freely scribbling the emotions of anger and sadness that can flood us at these times also helps.

Creating an altar honoring the person or pet is one option. Or make a collage with copies of photos and images that represent their life.

If you could have a conversation with someone you love who is no longer in your life, what would you need or want to say? Write a letter expressing this.

Red

I splash through puddles in my red boots,
Fireman boots, fire truck red.
I peel a carrot
Serrated edge to orange flesh,
And hear, a continent away,
The grind of gears,
The rumble of heavy machinery,
As jagged teeth on oversize buckets,
Comb the rubble,
Peeling, layer upon layer.

I find my cat's prey,
Disemboweled and halved.
Disgusted, dismayed
I curse this instinct,
Not even fancy feasts and soft love,
Can extinguish.

I say a prayer for lives lost.
This rabbit unsuspecting as he hopped his early morning rounds.
So close to the ground only a cat's eye could spot.
And the thousands high above ground
Moving routinely through early morning rituals
In twin towers of glass and steel,
So alien to my world.

And beyond to dark caves underground
Where plots hatch like monster eggs,
Where ideas not instincts
Demand the death of another.

My everyday motions almost irreverent
I light candles.
The glass reflects their flickering
Like tiny fires in prairie fields.
Primitive gestures,
Comfort in the dark wilderness.

Grief

PROCESS NOTES

I am going about my day with the awareness of the 9/11 tragedy in New York heavy on my mind. How to recognize that, give it a place and space rather than ignoring or repressing it? I do create an altar at home and at the inn, as some of our staff had lost relatives there. Spontaneously people add objects. We see this with memorials that spring up at the scene of accidents, shootings and kidnappings. Yellow ribbons keep the war and those fighting alive in our minds. These expressions give form and shape to our feelings. "The object of art is to give life shape," wrote Jean Anouilh.

While making dinner, the horrific images play in my mind. I see the rescue efforts, hear the machinery, imagine those combing through the rubble. Then I notice the reflection in the window of a candle I have burning for those affected, a tiny light in the black night sky.

I choose this image *Grief* done as a Soulcollage® card. The process is to write from the "I am" place. The voice of this card speaks:

"I am she who holds the light in the darkness of sorrow and loss. I am she who stares into the depths of despair with a ring of glowing candles surrounding me. Each holds someone's prayer. I am Grief. I remind that loving less, to soften this pain, is not an option."

PLAYTIME

Some questions you might explore with art making and writing:

Represent, with imagery, a helper who supports you in times of difficulty.

Or you might imagine a place or symbol of serenity. Express this through art making or writing.

You may have pieces of music that also offer comfort or song lyrics or lines from a poem. Collage those.

Honoring a loss through writing your memories of the person or situation also enriches and deepens your relationship to it.

Air

The shade on the window
   Breathes with the breeze
An irregular rhythm
In
Out.

It takes a while to isolate
The soft, unfamiliar sound
Not a whistle, not a tick
More a tap, a psst.

The ventilator
 Breathes for you now
Slowly, steadily
Up
Down.

I am not immediate family
Nor part of the most intimate ring
So have no access to your hospital bed.
I am allowed to light candles
Shed tears
Celebrate love
Mysterious connections.

I am allowed to stand before your silent house
"As lonely as a prom dress on the clearance rack."

They say the body is the house of the soul.
I'm sure those by your bedside know
You've slipped out through a cracked window
Off to the prom
With incredible beauty and grace
Your graduation day
Blowing a kiss good-bye
To us on this side
Creating
A soft breeze
That stirs the shade
Catches my attention
As I place the mail
You will never read
On the empty table.

Out the Window

Taking Off

PROCESS NOTES

"Air" starts with a mystery and ends with the Great Mystery. I am sitting and hear a subtle sound I can't immediately identify. The cloth window shade is blowing slightly, creating an unusual sound. A close friend's mother, who is also our neighbor, contracted an illness while on vacation and is dying. I am aware of the great shock and sadness surrounding those at the hospital. She is a beautiful woman. It is May. Someone who worked here used to say "I'm off, like a prom dress!" and I remember that I always wanted to use the line "as lonely as a prom dress on a clearance rack." Somehow these ideas ran together with my love of these people and my sense of exclusion. As I wrote, the idea of graduation worked its way in. The word "commencement" is always on the high school graduation program, as in beginnings, not endings. The image of a window is rich with meaning, an opening to other worlds, a passage between inner and outer.

I make two collages reflecting the imagery of the poem. The first, *Out the Window*, is very simple: just a cutout shape and an open window with a sheer curtain blowing. The shape suggests someone in a ballooning gown. The empty silhouette mirrors the space where something that was is no more, much like a police chalk outline. The other, *Taking Off*, contains more details: a perfume atomizer representing a breathing tube, the body leaving the hospital bed, off like a prom dress into the beyond. I wanted a picture of the window shade that first caught my attention and this is the closest I found. I felt a sense of liberation, celebration and expansion in looking at this, which balanced the heaviness of my sad heart.

Playtime

Some questions you might explore with art making and writing:

Try a sensory awareness exercise. Right where you are, begin to use your ears, your eyes, your nose, as fully as possible. Pretend you have never been where you are before. What do you notice? What grabs your attention? Perhaps you will journey somewhere new, as I did. Write or draw. Expand, amplify.

The collages I did in response to my poem changed my feelings and my thinking about the process of dying. Think of something that you judge as dark, scary, negative, ugly or somehow very off-putting and play with shifting it to its opposite value.

To the Very Heart/Onion Heart

I sat down
To draw a heart
And the page
In its infinite wisdom
Shows me an onion.
Onion heart.
The heart as onion
To be peeled
Through many layers
To reach
The heart of hearts
Tears streaming
All the while.

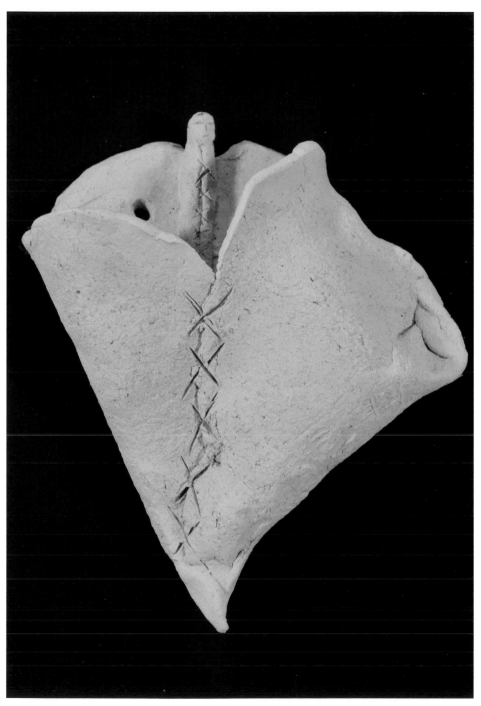

Heart Spirit

PROCESS NOTES

Drawing often reveals something unintended to me. I am not a trained artist, so this makes for surprises. In this case, the onion-shaped heart was perfect—exactly what I wanted. There is a process of un-layering that I need to move through in order to reach my innermost heart. There is no shortcut to wisdom or compassion. I have to feel my way, sense it as in Braille reading.

I was unable to find the drawing that inspired this poem. I recall the heart was lopsided and lined which suggested an onion. I choose this clay piece as it shows a heart that has been broken and stitched back together. Inside lies a spindle, a spirit of tender loving.

PLAYTIME

Some questions you might explore with art making and writing:

I once read that when women are angry they cry and when men are sad they act angry. Our emotions can bleed into one another and become camouflaged. Use color, shape and texture to portray different emotions.

Do your tears or rage have words?

Let your tears flow and see them as drops in the ocean of human suffering. Draw this.

Winter

I add the following collage of winter photographs done by a friend, Nancy J. Hall in the interest of balance. Having grown up in the Canadian Midwest (where Nancy still lives in the Interlake of Manitoba), I relate to the long, harsh winters foreign to my present life. Transplanted to Northern California, I took some time to detect subtle seasonal changes. The temperate climate felt like a continuous spring-fall combo.

The creative process can also be understood through the natural rhythms of the seasons. The expressive phase—spring—I cover in great length since I am encouraging this aspect, but it is important to honor the previous state—winter. For many, winter represents darkness, emptiness, bleakness: a black-and-white, lifeless world; frozen rivers and lakes; bare branches, structures buried beneath snowbanks; a daily struggle against brutal nature.

Yet we know winter allows the necessary incubation that renews and restores life. Seeds sleep, bears hibernate, long nights foster dreaming. Invisible forces are active. Our creative souls also need quiet times, to turn inward, to retreat. And when we experience fallow periods, we might be kinder to ourselves and view them as winter.

"Beneath winter's blanket, restless spring's shadow stirs." I wrote this during a time when I was frustrated and blocked to remind myself that my urges were seeds needing ripening.

Winter

PLAYTIME

Some questions you might explore with art making and writing:

What feelings do images of winter evoke?

Are there areas in your life that feel barren? What do they need?

Notice what winter symbolizes for you. Play with the images.

How do you relate to darkness? To loss?

What warms your heart and soul? What fire is in your belly?

Thinking of holiday celebrations: what do you find most meaningful? Are there special rituals or memories attached? Explore with writing or art making.

Shorter days and longer nights mean more time for dreaming. What is your relationship to you dreams?

Care and Cleaning Instructions
(Affixed to the Label on a Human Heart)

To remove pain stains from a broken heart,
(Works also for those stubborn, hard to remove stains
left from shattered dreams)
Soak in tears.
Not just overnight but for years.
Let stand.
Do not rub, scrub or agitate.
Wait.
Time and tears will do the job.
Place on windowsill,
Let sun and moon watch over (they teach of cycles).
Expose to soft, cool breezes,
Whose touch, felt but unseen,
Speaks in heart's tongue.
After some time, place heart in dark woods,
In sunny meadow,
Often by riverbank, seashore,
(the flowing on, the next wave, teach of healing).
Burn a candle, sage,
Sing a lullaby.
To test for doneness
Take heart to where children play,
A spring garden, near new lovers.

Wash on gentle cycle (a circle of women works wonders).

Dry, low heat, delicate.

Wear on sleeve.

Repeat as needed.

Heart Care-Taker

Shrine: She Who Tends to Wounded Hearts

PROCESS NOTES

While visiting my mother, who had dementia, I met a lady in the laundry room of their facility. I was grieving over the loss of my mother since her illness, and other heartaches, and was a little distracted while she talked. Then something made me pay attention and she shared some incredible stories. This conversation ended with hugs and tears. While sorting the clothes, I laughingly said, "Our hearts should come with care instructions!"

This led to some musings about the kind of instructions needed: how to assemble, how to use, precautionary disclaimers and repair hints. No doubt as with other kits, a critical piece would be missing and I would have to improvise anyway. Once fixing breakfast, I noticed on a carton, "to open, separate wings." I thought, " aha, a heart how-to." In a writing exercise titled "I gave my heart . . ." I played with giving my heart an ache without warming up properly, as in falling in love rashly. This poem resulted from all those ideas. This carved *Heart Care-taker*, is a good companion for it. I also created a little shrine *She Who Tends to Wounded Hearts*.

PLAYTIME

Some questions you might explore with art making and writing:

How do you care for your heart?

What makes your heart sing?

What makes your heart cry?

Create an image or an altar of your heart care-taker.

I Am She Who Holds the Moon in Her Belly

I am she who holds the moon in her belly
Earth
And
Sky Mother.
My hair creates the rolling mists.
My feet are planted in riverbed
Forest roots
The hidden half of the circle
Of these rounded hills.
I am she who holds the watery, misty worlds
The fullness of change.
My center waxes and wanes.
I am married to the darkness
With my ring of moonlight.

Circle Dancer

Process Notes

The collage *Circle Dancer* shows a woman completing the circle of heaven and earth. I see the landscape above ground and know there is more beneath the surface. I connect my cycles to the moon, recognizing the marriage of self to universals. More and more I see I am the bridge, the vertical axis, grounding the spiritual realm here on earth through my body.

Playtime

Some questions you might explore with art making and writing:

Stand firmly rooted to the ground. Extend your arms out wide to each side. Consider the cross symbol. There is a similar vertical and horizontal axis. Imagine the energy of the earth rising up through your feet and body and the energy of the universe coming in through you head and down. Imagine your hands connecting to others creating a social network. Create a collage or drawing of this.

I AM
(CHANT)

I am of the water, of the water, watch me flow-o-o-o.
Watch me rise, watch me fall
Like a wave, a snaking wave upon the water.

I am of the earth, of the earth, watch me grow-o-o-o.
Reaching down, underground, reaching up meeting sky
A waving, standing snake upon the earth.

I am of the sky, of the sky, watch me go-o-o-o.
Watch me fly, wings spread wide
Covering all, a winged snake flying high in the sky.

I am of the fire, of the fire, watch me glow-o-o-o.
Flaming higher, flaming higher
Burning red, burning orange
Burning, burning, burning
A rising snake of desire in the fire
I am of all these things
      Elemental
        Universal
          Everlasting
I am, I am, I am, I am, I am, I am . . .

Connector

PROCESS NOTES

This came to me as a chant. The words water, earth, sky, and fire are meant to be stressed with the "o" sounds rising up and down in tone. I had been working with images of snakes and felt this was about shedding skins and transformation. Exploring mythology, I also discovered the snake as the symbol of life and death, the head curling on itself to eat its tail. Again, the imagery of the poem speaks to my growing awareness of connection to the larger circle of life, the transpersonal realm. I am also feeling my aliveness.

The collage, *Connector*, represents this energetic exchange. I am reminded of the animating electrical current in monster films such as *Frankenstein* that brings a creature to life.

PLAYTIME

Some questions you might explore with art making and writing:

Create your own chant or theme song.

Represent the imagery with art.

Poem of Gratitude

I am grateful for:
The color yellow,
The smell of lilacs,
Shades of blue,
The moon,
Waxing and waning.
The sun, ah yes, the sun,
The color yellow.
The scent of roses,
The touch of their petals,
The ferocity of their thorns.
Green, the color green.
The flickering of the flame,
Red-orange in the fire.
The color yellow.
Tea in a yellow cup with roses.
The candle, like a paintbrush,
The point being to enlighten,
To delight, to enchant.
The fur on my cat,
The purr in his throat,
The breeze on my skin.
My skin.
My eyes, my legs, my heart.
This moment.

Giving Thanks

Aah, Spring!

Spring Breathes

Spring breathes green
Into the tips of trees,
Teases the wintry pout
Out of the air,
Kisses the buds, awakening them from beauty sleep:
"Welcome Princess Iris, Royal Rhododendron, this is your realm."

Spring paints
With Impressionistic daubs
This hillside, that field:
Lavender, rose, purple, red,
Yellow, orange, blue.
A few errant drops
Splatter my shoulder,
Dissolving,
Like fairy dust,
The chip lodged there.

Spring frolics
With lambs and chicks
Nestlings with scrawny necks
Baptizing all the newborns
With gentle tears.

Spring snickers all the way to summer,
Leaving me amid the blooms and babes,

A fevered child again,
Restless to be outdoors,
Delirious with color,
Burning up with life.

Dance in Green

PROCESS NOTES

Playing with word associations can become a poem. "My Slinky" is a lighthearted piece about spring energy. Free associating meanings of the word "spring" took me on a journey back to my childhood in Winnipeg. I recalled the exuberance and liberation that came with the thawing of frozen rivers and the removal of heavy overcoats and boots. I realized the universal significance, and power and promise, of spring symbols.

The collage *Aah, Spring!* captures the memory I have of getting dressed up and wearing patent leather shoes to celebrate Easter as a little girl. No more winter boots. I feel free and open my arms to receive the excitement of spring.

"Spring Breathes" also addresses the rebirth of this season. Like mouth-to-mouth resuscitation, the breath of spring revives us.

The collage *Dance in Green* is an exuberant celebration piece. I am joining with nature and the rebirthing energy of spring. Green is the color of growth and healing.

PLAYTIME

Some questions you might explore with art making and writing:

This is a lengthy section with more detailed instructions, as I find spring really represents the expressive side of transformation. What has rested dormant now bursts alive. Feel free to refer back to this section when following any other prompts.

Think of a symbol of spring. Close your eyes and imagine that as fully as possible, adding color, shape, scent, sound, and texture. For example, when imagining a robin, see the red breast, the feathers, hear the chirping, see the hopping. Allow this image to come alive. Now draw that using color and shape. It doesn't have to be a pictorial representation, simply depict the energy of the symbol or the feeling it evokes in you.

Notice how you feel in the process.

Now allow yourself to imagine you are that symbol and write a few sentences beginning, "I am . . ." For example, "I am robin . . ."

Notice if you recognize any associations to your own life. Write about them.

Spring is about birthing, moving from being held in to being released. When you are feeling confined, held in, or held back, what does that look like? Represent that with color and shape.

Now consider what breaking free would look like. What would represent freedom? Draw that. Write a few words about this experience.

Imagine yourself incubating in a protected place like a chrysalis. Draw that. Imagine yourself emerging. Who are you? Draw that. Write a few words about this process, how you feel in both states.

Spring is also about preparing the ground and planting seeds. Write a little about what seeds you want to plant. What do they need to grow? How can you provide these conditions? How will you recognize the first tender shoots? Create a collage on this theme.

I grew up in the Canadian Midwest where spring represented a liberation from the grip of a long, hard winter. When we shed our heavy coats and our boots, we felt pounds lighter. What has been weighing on you, that you can now shed? What does this "lighter" you feel like? Draw or collage this shift.

A classic concept of spring is emerging from a long winter's sleep, hibernation. A bear feels the warmth that heralds winter's end and stretches awake. He comes down the mountain hungry. Is there a dream that has been part of your winter's sleep that now wants to have a waking life? Is there a hidden hunger in you? Explore these ideas with drawing, collaging, or writing.

Easter egg hunts are another part of our spring rituals. A phrase that comes to mind is "Don't put all your eggs in one basket." We need to spread out possibilities, especially as we age. Just because we experience a loss doesn't mean that all is lost. An egg is also a container for what wants to be born. The ship might have sailed on some of our hopes and dreams but don't forget to check the other baskets. Playing with this metaphor, draw some egg shapes with possibilities inside.

"April is the cruellest month," wrote T.S. Eliott. Spring can be a difficult time when we feel disconnected from the exuberant mood of nature. When our hearts are heavy, the contrast feels too great; it may feel too much to ask of ourselves to rally that upbeat energy. If you are feeling this way, honor the validity of your emotions. Create an image, collage, or small story to hold this darker, perhaps nostalgic, energy.

In the spring a young man's fancy turns to love, so it is said. All around us there is mating and sexual energy. Frozen lakes and rivers thaw and flow again. Is there any hardened place in your heart that wants to soften? Write a love letter to yourself or to someone else.

Whisper/Moon Butterfly

I am a whisper in the ear of eternity,
    A butterfly in the forest of forever,
  A moonbeam in the light of love.

The invitation is to dance the spiral dance
Of life and loss, love and longing
As eyeless skulls watch
And toothless mouths grin beneath my feet.
To spin
As others circle and clap the beat
The rhythm of flame and heat.

The invitation is to swim with wings
Diving deep into the fire
Of breath and death,
To shatter the glass that shelters and confines
To unwind the cocoon,
To shed skin
To spread wings
To spin, to dance
To discover:
I am a whisper in the ear of eternity,
    A butterfly in the forest of forever,
  A moonbeam in the light of love.

Whisper in the Ear

PROCESS NOTES

The group I belonged to often began our sessions with a silent exercise. One evening we were asked to randomly and blindly select three words from a magnetic poetry board. Mine were "whisper," "moon," and "butterfly." The first three lines came to me as lines sometimes do, as from another dimension, as if they came through me. They carried weight and power. I didn't write anything further until after the evening ended. The imagery in the body of the poem refers to another woman's collage that she shared that night. Another member of the group wrote music to these words later in the year. I love this poem and its message. It became the inspiration and the original title for this book, *Whispers*. I feel the soul whispers to us all, that

> "We are a whisper in the ear of eternity,
> a butterfly in the forest of forever,
> a moonbeam in the light of love."

The collage *Whisper in the Ear* honors the muse or the voice of our inner self. I use butterflies often in my collages and they symbolize transformation, spirit, and fleeting beauty for me.

PLAYTIME

Some questions you might explore with art making and writing:

Sit quietly. Close your eyes. Allow images of beauty, peace, unfolding, grace, and infinity to emerge. Through writing or art making, let these images to speak to you.

Pick some words at random and let a poem or story evolve.

Creativity Collage

I am the one who through my hands
Releases seeds that grow into blooms.
I am the one who trusts in creative transformation
From chrysalis to butterfly.
I am the one who reminds
That my hands are needed
To birth the new.
I am the one who reminds
"Begin . . . continue."

Creativity

PROCESS NOTES

This last piece is another Soulcollage® card. I felt it fitting to conclude with the message that it spoke. I encourage you to explore your own creativity, as there is no other person in the entire world that can express what you can. Your hands and hearts are needed. To come full circle, I wish you the eyes of a child to see the world anew and the joy of creating as a child does. But even if you never make a drawing or write a poem, your creativity can shine in many areas of your life when you reclaim that original playful energy. The suggestions offered here are ways to reflect for a more meaningful connection to the moments of our ordinary lives.

May your journey be as blessed as mine continues to be.

Permissions

The author thanks the following for their permission to reprint from copyrighted works.

Stephen Nachmanovitch, for excerpts from *Free Play: The Power of Improvisation in Life and the Arts* © 1990 by Jeremy P. Tarcher, Inc.

Kate Donohue for the use of her image of a head used in my collage *Reality*.

Santa Clara Magazine for excerpts from an interview with Fr. William Rewak, author of *The Right Taxi*, in Winter 2013 issue.

Parallax Press, for an excerpt from *Present Moment, Wonderful Moment: Mindfulness Verses for Daily Living* by Thich Nhat Hanh, 1990, www.parallax.org.

Footnotes

1. (Page 42) Pat Allen writes about the importance of stating an intention in both *Art Is a Way of Knowing* (1995) and *Art Is a Spiritual Path* (2005). In fact, the first chapter in her 2005 book, which begins on p. 11, is "The Practice of Intention."
2. (Page 45) Mary Oliver, *New and Selected Poems*, 1992, p. 10.
3. (Page 46) Stephen Nachmanovitch, *Free Play*, 1999, p. 158.
4. (Page 47) Fr. William Rewak in an interview in *Santa Clara Magazine*, winter 2013, pp. 28–29.
5. (Page 55) Mark Nepo, *Seven Thousand Ways to Listen*, 2012, p. 5 and p. 12.
6. (Page 83) Joan Halifax, *The Fruitful Darkness: Reconnecting with the Body of the Earth*, 1993, pp. 204–205 quoting from *Present Moment, Wonderful Moment*, 1990, by Thich Nhat Hanh, Parallax Press, Berkeley, CA
7. (Page 94) Antoine de Saint-Exupery, *The Little Prince*, 1943, p. 70.
8. (Page 137) Marianne Williamson, *A Return to Love*, 1992, p. 190.
9. (Page 162) Some of my collages are done as Soulcollage® cards. See Seena B. Frost, *Soulcollage®: An Intuitive Collage Process for Individuals and Groups*, Santa Cruz, CA: Hanford Mead Publishers Inc., 2001.

Suggestions for Further Readings

There are many books that teach techniques, great resources when you are exploring different media. And great for inspiration! Trying new things means we have more tools to play with. I encourage you to experiment playfully.

There are also many books that address art therapy and play therapy, if you want to delve more deeply into the roots and theory of these fields. My short list: Pat Allen, Shaun McNiff, Bruce Moon, Lucia Capacchione, Violet Oaklander, Linda Chapman and James Hillman.

Remember, inspiration can be found anywhere, not just in a book: on a walk, in a thrift store, a hardware store, an art supply store, a bookstore reading, a museum or a gallery. I find conversations with children are often refreshing in their literal interpretations and their appreciation of the simplest things.

Similarly, poets open our eyes to the ordinary, to the timelessness in the temporal. I discovered some of my favorites browsing in bookstores or found quoted in novels. My short list: Naomi Shihab Nye, Mary Oliver, David Whyte, Sharon Olds, Billy Collins, Mark Nepo, Marge Piercy, Seamus Heaney and Thich Nhat Hahn.

For motivation re writing, Brenda Ueland (*If You Want to Write*), Laura Deutsch (*Writing From the Senses*) and Natalie Goldberg (*Writing Down the Bones, Wild Mind*). Many authors address journaling.

I am a great believer in following your nose re finding books that inspire. I often feel that titles find me. My shelves are overstuffed with many genres: novels, nonfiction, as well as those on creativity and spirituality. It is hard to pick, but here is a short list:

Lucia Capacchione, *The Creative Journal: The Art of Finding Yourself*, 1980, Newcastle Pub Co, Hollywood, California.

Patti Digh, *Life Is a Verb*, 2008, and *Creative Is a Verb*, 2010, Skirt/Globe Pequot Press, Guilford, Connecticut.

Seena B. Frost, *SoulCollage®*, 2001, and *SoulCollage® Evolving*, 2010, Hanford Mead Publishers Inc., Santa Cruz, California.

Sheri Gaynor, *Creative Awakenings*, 2009, North Light Books, Cincinnati, Ohio.

Corita Kent and Jan Steward, *Learning by Heart*, 1992, Bantam Books, New York, New York.

Austin Kleon, *Steal Like an Artist*, 2012, Workman, New York, New York.

Jan Phillips, *Marry your Muse*, 1997, and *Finding The On-Ramp to Your Spiritual path,* 2013, Quest Books, Wheaton, IL.

Kelly Rae Roberts, *Taking Flight*, 2008, North Light Books, Cincinnati, Ohio.

Sharon Soneff, *Art Journals and Creative Healing*, 2008, Quarry Books, Beverly, Massachusetts.

Acknowledgments

I owe a debt to those who have inspired me. Marilyn Hagar—mentor, friend and collaborator—for creating the space for me to discover ways to express myself; all the fellow explorers in the art groups here and at SSU; Suzanne Lovell, mother of us all in the art therapy program at SSU, for insisting I stop simply quoting sources and discover my own wisdom; my students and clients, for teaching me; Robbie Engelmann, friend and soul sister, cheerleader extraordinaire; Nancy Hall, friend since kindergarten, a true renaissance woman; Jill Titus, friend, fellow explorer and teacher; Dana Ecelberger, another fellow explorer, a creative spirit living her life out loud. Always my children, Alex and Kate, who first reminded me to play, and Jeff, my steadfast partner, who supports me in so many ways.

To Toni Bernbaum, for helping with the poems, and Kate Doughtery, for reading the first draft; as both artists and poets, their insights were invaluable; Adrienne Ardito and Sid Garza-Hillman, for photographing the images, and Sid also for tech tutoring; Doreen Schmid for being the right editor; and finally, the team at She Writes Press, for giving the book a chance. Heartfelt thanks to you all for being in my life.

And finally to Carl Jung, whose work continues to inspire so many to journey within, to explore images as a path to wholeness and authenticity.

About the Author

J oan Stanford is a board-certified art therapist and full-time innkeeper who has been facilitating creativity groups for over twenty years encouraging people of all ages, especially non-artists, to expand their awareness through playing with art materials. She has been recognized with the Soroptimist "Making a Difference For Women" award for an art-based curriculum she co-created and taught in local schools. Her poems have been published and her art exhibited. She lives in Mendocino with her husband, and offers imagination playshops and creativity retreats at their inn and wellness center. Her website is www.joanstanford.com.

photo by Sid Garza-Hillman

Selected Titles from She Writes Press

She Writes Press is an independent publishing company founded to
serve women writers everywhere. Visit us at www.shewritespress.com.

Think Better. Live Better. 5 Steps to Create the Life You Deserve by Francine Huss.
$16.95, 978-1-938314-66-7. With the help of this guide, readers will learn to cultivate
more creative thoughts, realign their mindset, and gain a new perspective on life.

The Thriver's Edge: Seven Keys to Transform the Way You Live, Love, and Lead by
Donna Stoneham. $16.95, 978-1-63152-980-1. A "coach in a book" from master ex-
ecutive coach and leadership expert Dr. Donna Stoneham, The Thriver's Edge outlines
a practical road map to breaking free of the barriers keeping you from being everything
you're capable of being.

Journey of Memoir: The Three Stages of Memoir Writing by Linda Joy Myers. $22.95,
978-1-938314-26-1. A straightforward, highly effective workbook designed to help
memoirists of every level get their story on the page.

*Stop Giving it Away: How to Stop Self-Sacrificing and Start Claiming Your Space,
Power, and Happiness* by Cherilynn Veland. $16.95, 978-1-63152-958-0. An empow-
ering guide designed to help women break free from the trappings of the needs, wants,
and whims of other people—and the self-imposed limitations that are keeping them
from happiness.

Renewable: One Woman's Search for Simplicity, Faithfulness, and Hope by Eileen
Flanagan. $16.95, 978-1-63152-968-9. At age forty-nine, Eileen Flanagan had an ach-
ing feeling that she wasn't living up to her youthful ideals or potential, so she started
trying to change the world—and in doing so, she found the courage to change her life.

Hedgebrook Cookbook: Celebrating Radical Hospitality by Denise Barr & Julie Ro-
sten. $24.95, 978-1-938314-22-3. Delectable recipes and inspiring writing, straight
from Hedgebrook's farmhouse table to yours.